Easter People

Easter People
Living Community

LUIS ANTONIO G. (CHITO) TAGLE

ORBIS BOOKS
Maryknoll, New York 10545

Founded in 1970, Orbis Books endeavors to publish works that enlighten the mind, nourish the spirit, and challenge the conscience. The publishing arm of the Maryknoll Fathers and Brothers, Orbis seeks to explore the global dimensions of the Christian faith and mission, to invite dialogue with diverse cultures and religious traditions, and to serve the cause of reconciliation and peace. The books published reflect the views of their authors and do not represent the official position of the Maryknoll Society. To learn more about Maryknoll and Orbis Books, please visit our website at www.maryknoll.org.

Copyright © 2005 by Luis Antonio G. Tagle

Published by Orbis Books, Maryknoll, New York 10545-0308.
Manufactured in the United States of America.

All rights reserved. No part of this publication may be reproduced or transmitted in any form or by any means, electronic or mechanical, including photocopying, recording or any information storage or retrieval system, without prior permission in writing from the publisher.

Queries regarding rights and permissions should be addressed to: Orbis Books, P.O. Box 308, Maryknoll, New York 10545-0308.

Scripture quotations are from the *Christian Community Bible*, 31st edition, copyright © 2000 by Bernardo Hurault and published by Claretian Publications, U.P.P.O. Box 4, 1101 Quezon City, Philippines. Used by permission. All rights reserved.

Grateful acknowledgment is made to the Loyola School of Theology at Ateneo de Manila University in Quezon City, Philippines, the publisher of *It Is the Lord: Occasional Lectures at Loyola Schoool of Theology* (copyright © 2003 Loyola School of Theology) and to the Jesuit Communications Foundation, Inc., at Ateneo de Manila University in Quezon City, Philippines, the publisher of *An Easter People: Our Christian Vocation To Be Messengers of Hope* (copyright © 2003 Luis Antonio G. Tagle).

Library of Congress Cataloging-in-Publication Data

Tagle, Luis Antonio.
    Easter people : living community / Luis Antonio (Chito) Tagle.
    p. cm.
    ISBN 1-57075-596-5 (pbk.)
    1. Church. 2. Community—Religious aspects—Catholic Church. 3. Catholic Church—Doctrine. I. Title.
BX1746. T34 2005
262—dc22

                                  2004023786

Contents

Acknowledgments   7

Introduction: The Disillusionment of Our Time   9

1. Living Christian Community—A Sign of Faith   15

2. The Path to Community   33

3. A Community of Love   47

4. A Community of Solidarity   59

5. Praying Together   75

6. A Community of Hope   89

7. A Community of the Holy Spirit   99

8. Reaching Out   113

About the Author   *125*

Acknowledgments

This book on Christian community is itself a product of community, of many people who worked together. Most of the materials gathered in this small volume came from lectures I delivered at the Loyola School of Theology, Philippines, on different occasions, and retreats preached at different times to the Philippines Provinces of the Religious of the Good Shepherd and the Congregation of Our Lady of the Retreat in the Cenacle. I thank the administration, the teaching and non-teaching staff, and the students of Loyola School of Theology and the religious women of the two congregations for being such wonderful companions in faith and in the journey of hope.

I also thank my ecclesial community in the Diocese of Imus—the edifying laypeople, the inspiring presbyterium, the caring religious, the encouraging seminarians, and the stirring yet disturbing poor in our midst. I would not have dared to talk about community if I had not experienced its joys and struggles among the great people of our diocese. With them I hear clearly the call to the Church to be community in our uncertain times.

My family, the church community in our household, has always been a bastion of faith, hope, and love for me. I thank God for initiating me into the process of achieving community through my parents and brother, my aunts, uncles, and cousins, who untiringly weave a sturdy web of love for every member of the family, especially for me, to feel secure and loved.

I also acknowledge the scholars, writers, and teachers who have helped form my theological and pastoral vision, but whose names

I did not always mention in the book. To this community of theologians, pastors, and people of prayer, I am grateful. My thanks also go to the kind-hearted and patient Mary Ann Charity Durano, who edited the original lectures and conferences for their publication in the Philippines. I want to say a special word of thanks to Michael Leach for encouraging me to pursue this project with Orbis Books. And I could go on and on telling everyone about Susan Perry, my editor at Orbis. She did for me more than what duty called for. Through the different stages of this project, I never felt alone. She provided me with the sense of community needed by anyone to accomplish anything worthwhile.

Finally to the Triune God, mystery of communion in mission, may praise and honor be!

Introduction: The Disillusionment of Our Time

This is the age of globalization, when boundaries are being broken down, when people fly from Tokyo to New York City or from Manila to Los Angeles for a meeting, and when books are written in one country, submitted by e-mail to a second country, and printed in a third. It is a time when the same films are being viewed in Bombay, Chicago, and London, and young people in San Francisco, Brooklyn, Hong Kong, Johannesburg, and Berlin wear the same style of clothes. Indian curry is served in Milan, Neapolitan pizza in Shanghai, and Japanese tempura in Frankfurt. Korean and Taiwanese entrepreneurs manage transnational corporations in Manila, while Filipinos labor in oil companies in Kuwait, in households in Italy, and in hospitals in England. Are we seeing the beginnings of a new human family where barriers are torn down?

As people and ideas move swiftly around the globe, so does capital, as our economies are also globalized. But, of course, the transfer of capital is true only for those who are already economically strong. They have the capital to transfer and they do not need to fear boundaries. This holds true only for large companies and wealthy individuals. It does not work for the owner of a small store or a small company, or for laborers or subsistence farmers. The power of money determines who can break through any wall. For the powerless poor the walls separating them from the rich are as high and thick as before. Authors like Nicanor Perlas rightly call the globalization we are experiencing "elite globalization" or "neo-liberal globalization."

Elite globalization has done little for the continuing exclusion of the poor. Even with all the technological and scientific progress that produces better food, provides people with cures, and makes life more comfortable, much has not changed for the poor. They remain poor. The only change is that the poor have grown in number. Many poor people have just resigned themselves to the reality that their children, and their children's children, will not be better off than they are right now. Their lack of hope is painful.

And exclusion continues—not only of the materially poor, but also of the socially and culturally poor. The crucifixion of the poor is a daily occurrence in our third millennium. With all the sophisticated weapons and arms that we have, this crucifixion could even lead to the annihilation of the whole human family and of the environment in which we live.

Yet, the form of globalization that alarms me the most is the globalization of culture. There seems to be a neo-liberal culture that is being exported and that is now being proposed as *the* unifying element: the culture that will unify humanity, the culture that will provide communion, the culture that will form us into men and women who will somehow understand one another. A Filipino Jesuit once pointed out that the global culture that is being exported and bought uncritically by many is no longer inspired by religious values. This global culture is quite neo-pagan in inspiration, influenced too by post-modern values—very secular, very individualistic, very competitive and very materialistic.

Two other aspects of the culture developing in the present millennium are suspicion and irreverence. People everywhere are suspicious of institutions that have failed to deliver what people expect from them. They are losing trust in families, governments, the military, financial institutions, and even the clergy. Suspicion is manifested often through irreverence. Irreverence could be prophetic but it can also deprive life of mystery. Everything is demythologized or explained away. The sense of the sacred is disappearing or gone. Gone also are the days when people walking along Roxas Boulevard in Manila, as they approached the Shrine of Our Mother of Perpetual Help, would stop their chatting momentarily and make the sign of the cross.

Notice also the dissipation of human energy. This disturbs me because I see this even among the young. I detect this when I give conferences to young people, students, seminarians, and even deacons who are about to be ordained priests. After the first fifteen minutes of my sharing, they get restless, unfocused and tired. They look like they have already lost their energy when I am just beginning to harness mine. I cannot determine whether the problem is with me or with them. How do we account for this loss of energy? Is it due to the pollution of the environment, unhealthy food, or the stressful speed of life? Are we oppressed by unreachable expectations and goals?

One indication of this low energy level is boredom. Young people seem to get bored so early in life. They have not yet lived enough but they are already bored with life. To remedy the boredom, they create—according to them—a lot of "gimmicks," or according to the young priests, "happenings," or, in the words of the once-were-young, "rackets." People are constantly looking for something new. For me, the best symbol of this desire, this constant shifting of attention, is the remote control for the television.

Shifting has been made comfortable, effortless. In a short span of time, you can see so many shows without beginning anything at the beginning, without ending anything at the end, and this is what we call relaxation or recreation. My worry is that, apparently, the solution to the dissipation of energy and boredom is to be content with bits and pieces, even if these are not connected in a meaningful whole. People are getting used to life as segments that may not be interconnected with one another. What I fear is that people will start thinking like this: A complete life is a boring life; a complete story is a boring story. An interesting story, an interesting life, is a life that has had numerous shifts. Wholeness and integration are nice words but they cost a person too much energy to achieve. Is it worth the effort? Unity of life is no longer a goal. It makes life boring. It means our attention span and our excitement with life are confined to one segment.

Reflecting on this boredom, I ask: What gives energy? What gave our parents energy? What gave a Martin Luther King Jr. the energy to fight and to die?

Vision. Dreams. Most of the world remembers Martin Luther King Jr.'s "I have a dream." When there are dreams, when there are powerful, gripping dreams, we always have energy to spare. We can always find some silent, dark nook in our hearts where we will find some new spring of life and energy. But those are discovered when we have a vision, when we have dreams. The person with vision will have something to die for, something to offer one's life for, and if one has something to die for, then one has something to live for. One will have energy to die and, of course, one will have energy to live.

I remember the late Bishop Felix Paz Perez, the second bishop of the Diocese of Imus, one of my beloved predecessors. Before he suffered a fatal heart attack, he prepared a reflection for a group of seminarians that he was not able to deliver. Someone found his retreat notes and on the first page were the words: "The reason for my dying is the Jesus whom I love and the people whom I have loved. And therefore, the reason for my living is the same Jesus and the people whom I have loved." He was a man of vision. He would willingly die. He would have the energy to die. It bothers me when I see people, especially young people, without energy. My fear is that we might be facing a millennium where people do not have compelling visions or dreams and therefore might have no energy.

What are the dreams of our people now? No more than to own the latest cell phone? I was talking with a young woman who had just graduated from college. I asked her, "What is your dream in life?" "Father, my dream is I want to have the best cell phone available." You call that a dream? If that is a dream, you will not have energy, for that is not the type of dream that will stir in us the flames of energy.

I hope I am mistaken in my fear of a millennium without a clear engaging vision for our generation and the next. This lack of vision leads to a kind of violence committed by people who are frustrated and bored. They grasp for control in their desire to engineer the kind of life they would like to have, a life that may be beyond their reach, but a life they do not even dare to envision. This vision-less search brings forth tiredness, tiredness gives birth to frustration, and frustration breeds violence. This violence is coupled with intolerance of the other, which is a very puzzling thing. At a time when globalization is being sold to us—as one humanity, no more frontiers, no more boundaries, a global culture, a global civilization, a global economy—we become more and more intolerant of one another, and it is usually the "others" who become scapegoats for the ills that we find in our society. We do not want to admit that life is becoming meaningless. We do not even have the energy to understand it. It is convenient to just blame "the others" for whatever goes wrong. This happens among members of families, neighbors living in the same block, and the relations between nations.

Is this a very dark description of the millennium? Yes, but at the same time, as in the past lessons that we learned as church, it is usually in those dark unsettling moments when the Spirit blows mightily. The Spirit is the Spirit of hope. This millennium is a millennium not only of ambiguities and uncertainties, but also of promise and hope—hope in the search for a new humanity, the search for a new way of being human and being a human family.

So what do we do? Where do we turn? Where will our faith in Christ lead us?

1

Living Christian Community — A Sign of Faith

The Christian faith offers a vision of life, a vision of humanity, a vision of what we could become in Jesus Christ. In a time of disillusionment, we turn to our faith to awaken our drooping spirits and to find renewed vigor in our search for fullness of life. How does our faith in Jesus, the crucified yet Risen Lord, enable us to face a fragmented world? What does our faith have to offer? One contribution Christians can make is the recovery of the value of community in a divided world.

I have titled this book *Easter People: Living Community* because Easter is a great season of hope. Hope, which can lead to visions and dreams, seems to be the most essential element of community. Community is also a powerful sign of hope to a shattered world. We live in a time and in a world where signs of despair abound. Our life is marked by fragmentation, exclusion, violence, and destruction in families, neighborhoods, nations, and the whole world. Women and men of our time therefore yearn for true communities where they can experience peace and wholeness. The Easter event, Jesus' triumph over sin and death, gives us a new lease on life. We hope that as an Easter people we can share the light of Easter to dispel the darkness of alienation that has covered the world. Faith in the Risen Lord can be an impetus to live as community. In fact the first Christian community was born from the faith in the Risen Christ.

As a Christian community we must rediscover, recapture, and re-appropriate the power of Easter, this central element of our faith—hope in the coming forth of new life—which is the most powerful symbol of the faith that can transform our lives, our church, our nation and world. By going back to accounts of Easter in Scripture, we hope to see with renewed clarity how faith in the Risen Lord brings forth community.

After the arrest of Jesus in the Garden of Gethsemane, his disciples scattered. Fear probably pushed them into hiding. Frustrated with themselves, and even with Jesus, they must have lost their earlier zeal to work together for the liberation of Israel. Jesus' mission had failed. They had failed him too as friends and followers. They lost their direction. They were separated from each other.

How did the scattered disciples find their way to one another again? What gathered them again as a community? It was their common belief in the Risen Lord who appeared to them. His words were not of condemnation but of peace. He manifested himself to them not to judge but to forgive. The communion shattered by infidelity and selfishness was healed and restored by the one who has triumphed over sin and death. The Risen Lord had gathered them again. Their common experience of having seen the Lord and their common confession of the Risen Jesus as the Christ brought them together as a community of faith.

This re-gathering was sealed by the gift of the Holy Spirit who would continue to teach the disciples about Jesus. Thus the Spirit would keep alive the disciples' faith in Jesus and communion with him. In this way the Spirit animated the early Christian communities. And the Spirit continues to enliven Christian communities anywhere and at any time by inspiring faith and communion among the followers of Christ. As the Risen Jesus once gathered again his dejected disciples by manifesting the power of mercy and reconciliation over human failure and infidelity, so the Holy Spirit will always gather men and women who believe in the Risen Lord. The community of believers in Christ is a sign of hope to a world in search of true communion.

The Power of the Resurrection

> *On the Sabbath the women rested according to the commandment, but the first day of the week, at dawn, they went to the tomb with the perfumes and ointments they had prepared. Seeing the stone rolled away from the opening of the tomb, they entered and were puzzled to find that the body of the Lord Jesus was not there.*
>
> *Two men in dazzling garments appeared beside them. In fright the women bowed to the ground. But the men said, "Why look for the living among the dead? (You won't find him here. He is risen.) Remember what he told you in Galilee, that the Son of Man had to be given into the hands of sinners, be crucified, and rise on the third day." And they recalled Jesus' words.*
>
> *Returning from the tomb, they informed the Eleven and their companions. Among the women who brought the news were Mary Magdalene, Joanna, and Mary the mother of James. But however much they insisted, those who heard did not believe the seemingly nonsensical story. Then Peter got up and ran to the tomb. All he saw there on bending down were the linen cloths. He went home wondering.* (Luke 24:1–12)

The resurrection is a simple story, but in its simplicity the resurrection does not lose its power to penetrate our hearts and to renew us from within. Luke describes the women as returning "at daybreak," a manifestation of their eagerness to give loving service to their Lord Jesus. Not finding what they expected, the women were perplexed and afraid. In addition, the women nearly missed the miracle of the resurrection because they were forgetful, not recalling the words Jesus had spoken earlier. The angels had to tell them, "Remember what he said to you while he was still in Galilee, that the Son of Man must be handed over to sinners and be crucified, and rise on the third day" (Luke 24:6–7). The women were looking for the wrong thing because they did not remember.

In its simplicity the resurrection involves a question of memory and forgetfulness. Faith in the Risen Lord involves a movement from forgetfulness to memory. For us, the resurrection experience comes to life again as we remember Jesus, a remembering that elicits not only memories, but also gratitude and hope. St. James writes that our problem is forgetfulness when it comes to doing the will of God. We are "hearers of the word" but we forget what we hear; because of this, we do not do what we have heard. For James, failing to do the will of God is a question of forgetfulness, of not keeping in mind what we have heard from Jesus: "Be doers of the Word and not just hearers, lest you deceive yourselves. The hearer who does not become a doer is like that one who looked at oneself in the mirror. He looked and then promptly forgot what he was like" (James 1:22–24). We forget ourselves and we forget Jesus. We Filipinos love to sing, "*Maalaala mo kaya?*" (Will you remember?) Could it be that Jesus is serenading us with that song?

Memory and remembering are important in recognizing the truth of the resurrection. Remembering what Jesus taught and promised enables us to rise above the signs of death around us. The challenge before us is to keep the resurrection alive by keeping the memory of Jesus alive. For us Christians, the Christian life, which is the life of the resurrection, rests on remembrance. This is not a matter of simply recalling an idea or a concept. Rather it is keeping the presence of love alive in us.

Keeping the memory of Jesus alive also means remembering how God vindicated Jesus, a victim of injustice. Thus the resurrection involves keeping the memory of other victims alive, those whom the world wants to bury and forget. Such memory disturbs because it reminds us of human cruelty toward neighbors. But it is also a troubling memory because it contains the promise of God's mighty justice that is hope for victims but a menace to the unscrupulous. No wonder we choose to forget the victims of the past and of the present. Denial, cover-up, or selective memory soothe our consciences. One sure way of killing hope and the new life ushered in by the resurrection experience is by painting a rosy picture as if nothing bad had happened. As if there were no victims. As if there were no sin, no violence, no death. The moment we reach that point of denial and are anesthetized from the realities around us, then we have forgotten, and the resurrection no longer makes sense. Forgetfulness convinces us that God has not reversed sin and death.

When the women remembered, they returned to the eleven disciples and the others and announced what the angels had told them. The power of memory seized the women. From fearful confused disciples they became eager bearers of the Good News. In Greek the phrase reads, the women "kept telling" the eleven and the others. If we use our imagination, what the women did makes sense. When we have news that is truly good, we cannot simply receive it and keep it to ourselves. Eagerness bubbles within us to share it with others and not only once, but to keep telling the same good news over and over again. If something good is happening in our life and we decide to keep quiet about it, eventually we will not be able to help ourselves from telling someone about it, not always in words but often in smiles, goodness, and generosity. The joy we feel just exudes from within. And how much better if the news we bring is the heart of the Gospel! The Lord is risen! It is such good news that we cannot help but be eager and passionate in our proclamation.

A true evangelizer is so caught up in the beauty of the Good News that he or she is energized by it to proclaim it to others. If we feel timid and shy, perhaps the fundamental and deeper question to ask is, "Am I convinced that the news I bear is good?" First and foremost, "Is it good news for me? Do I remember the hope it offers to me and to the world? Am I fascinated by what I remember?" Maybe you do not see it as good news and so you are not excited. You might get more excited about midnight sales at a shopping center. Yet, we should not be naïve in thinking that our exuberance in bearing the Good News is a guarantee that we are indeed bringing the Good News. External fervor should spring from a heart captivated by what it remembers. And those who truly remember are able to discern if we are proclaiming the Gospel of Jesus or not.

While I was still studying in Washington, D.C., I went to a Jesuit priest to ask if I could go to him regularly for spiritual direction. A priest committed to action for social justice, Father Peter Henriot told me that during a Mass when the Gospel reading for the day was the Beatitudes, he pronounced, "Jesus said, 'Blessed are the rich for theirs is the kingdom of heaven; blessed are those laughing for they shall be comforted; blessed are the proud for they shall inherit; blessed are those who are full and not thirsty. . . .'" Halfway through the reading, he saw the congregation looking at each other, murmuring, "Something's wrong with the Gospel." He stopped and said, "What? So you know that what I am proclaiming is *not* the Good News. Now, we will listen to the Good News."

We cannot fool people. They know if the news we bring is indeed the Good News. From a logical standpoint, an individual can accept the proclamation, "Blessed are the rich, blessed are those who are happy, blessed are the proud, blessed are the full and not hungry." This is logical in that one can understand why those who are rich are blessed, but in the deepest recesses of their hearts, hearts touched by the gift of the Holy Spirit so that they would remember, people know that this is not *the* Good News. We are being invited by the resurrection witness of the women to make sure that we are bearers of the Good News. As true and good evangelizers, we remember and proclaim the Good News with exuberance, passion and joy.

It saddens me when seminarians, priests, religious, and lay leaders talk easily about so many different things, but when it comes to the joy of sharing the Good News with one another or with others they hesitate. Some readily talk about ideals and the lives of other people, but find it difficult to share their personal experiences of the Good News of the Risen One. I hope that the resurrection happens in our midst in the form of seminarians, priests, religious, and lay people able to share their personal experiences of the Good News with one another because they remember Jesus fondly and faithfully.

Communicating memories of the resurrection forges bonds of communion between persons. Memories of love's triumph over hatred, forgiveness over revenge, caring over indifference are memories of the Risen Lord. When shared sincerely and passionately, a community of shared memory and shared hope emerges.

Before returning to the Philippines after studying in the United States, I met a Chinese student from the People's Republic of China, where he was a student of sociology and economics. He was in Washington, D.C., to attend a conference. While he was at The Catholic University, the Tiananmen Square Massacre happened and he decided not to go home. He found a way for his wife to join him, and they stayed in Washington where he continued his studies. Despite being a non-believer who grew up without belonging to any religion, he was very interested in religions, especially Christianity. When he heard I was going back to the Philippines, he invited me to meet his wife and have supper with them.

He mentioned that he was enjoying his stay at the university and I asked if he was learning anything about religion and Christianity. "What is your impression of our faith, our religion?" "You know, your Bible is the most beautiful book I have ever read," he said. "How about the Christian approach to life? Have you had a chance to reflect on it?" "Yes," he said, "I have taken courses in Christian ethics, Christian doctrine, and history of Christian dogma." Then he said, "I think Christianity has solutions to all the problems of the world. If Christianity could only be lived out, all the problems that I see in China could be solved." And so I asked, "Are you a believer now?" His response was, "Not yet. My mind understands and my mind has decided that what I understand is true; but I still cannot say, 'I believe.'"

I found this Chinese student to be very, very wise. To make the jump from "This is true" to "I believe" is not just a matter of explication. There are many truths that we see, but to be able to say, "I believe" needs grace. I have a feeling that he already believes. I cannot believe that grace is absent. What else is missing for him to be able to say in grace, "I believe"?

Before we parted I told him, "Should you reach a point when you can say, 'I believe,' I hope you won't forget the Catholic tradition." He had mentioned that he also studied the Protestant tradition. "Oh, yes. I appreciate the many different traditions. Your Catholic tradition is much fuller," he said, adding, "but after two years here at Catholic University, my only heartache is that no Catholic priest, sister, or student has approached me to teach me about the Word of God. Every Friday the Baptists come to my house and invite me to learn about their religion. You Catholics are very, very weak in evangelism." As he said this I felt like a culprit. I realized that he was searching for a community that would share its faith, its memory with him. And somehow we failed him. A non-believer who spoke beautifully about the Word of God and the Catholic tradition was making me realize how my indifference, inaction, and sin of omission, in other words my failure to forge community with him, were turning me into an enemy of the Christian faith. Forgetfulness hindered me from actively building bridges of communion with him.

I still remember one of my professors saying that there is an unbeliever within every believer and that we need to constantly dialogue with, evangelize, and convert that part of us. Our belief in the resurrection rests in our acceptance of the cross of Jesus' love. The more we distance ourselves from the cross and push it to forgetfulness, the more the resurrection becomes a distant reality in our lives. Only by carrying the cross of the victims of history and society in love do we become agents of hope in society.

For us Christians the Eucharist is a special moment to gather in order to remember Jesus' crucified love and his glorious resurrection. We are also confirmed in our hope that the poor, lame, blind, and the least will sit at the eternal banquet with Christ. The Eucharist memorial makes the church really the Body of Christ. St. Augustine rightly says, "You, people of God, be what you receive. You received the Body of Christ. You are the Body of Christ. Be what you receive. Be what you celebrate." The Eucharist comes alive when the community that celebrates breaks both the Word and the Bread together around the one table of the Body of Christ and around the one table of human life. No ritual fully makes us the body of Christ. Only when we engage in the slow and painful process of making our human community the living Body of Christ do we make our gathering around the table of the Lord a meaningful reception of the body of Christ. But how do we form "community"? What do we understand by the word "community?" What makes a community worthy of calling itself the manifestation or the living remembrance of the Word and the presence of the Risen Christ?

What Is Community?

At this point, we will leave the scriptural stories of Easter for a while in order to reflect on the meaning of community. We will borrow insights from psychology and social theory. A community is very different from a group. Many groups exist but only a few communities; only a small number of groups are willing to make the transition from being a group to being a community. A group is a collection of people doing the same thing or who happen to be in the same place at the same time. A mere group cannot be the manifestation of the presence of the Risen Christ. On the other hand, a community is defined by the quality of presence among the members of a group.

We have the birth of a community when members in a group make the decision and commitment *to give the gift of a caring presence to each other*. No human community attains the status of community by chance. It requires a conscious decision and commitment on the part of each individual to offer to each other a quality of presence that is nurturing and caring. There is an old song written by Burt Bacharach and made famous by Dionne Warwick that describes the difference between a house and a home ("a chair is not a house and a house is not a home when there's no one there"). The difference between a house and a home is the difference between a group and a community ("a house is not a home when the two of us are far apart").

A community is also something we try to achieve but are never fully able to do so. The moment a group feels that it has reached the final stage of being a community and says, "Well, we are already a community" is the beginning of the end of that community. A community is always a work in progress. It is an experience that we always try to keep alive and real in our midst. It is an event. According to Jesuit theologian Bernard Lonergan, a community is born when there is an achievement of common meaning. The achievement comes in different kinds and degrees. For an event of common meaning to occur, people in that group first must have a *common field of experience*. The moment people do not have the time to share their experiences or let their experiences interact, it becomes difficult to create a community. Being out of a common field of experience is to be out of touch.

When I left the Philippines in 1985 for graduate studies abroad, a former student of mine sent me letters once a week and I wrote back every week. There was not a week when I did not know what was happening in his life, and a week did not go by when I did not tell him what was happening in mine. In one sense, our constant sharing enabled us to have a common field of experience. Then the letters started arriving every two weeks, and then once a month, once a semester, once a year—in the end, a Christmas card with no message, just "Merry Christmas." He got tired and so did I. Finally there were no more cards.

After seven years I returned to the Philippines. It was very awkward when we saw each other again. I could not even start a conversation. It seemed like we had nothing in common to talk about. We had lost touch with each other. When I saw him I said, "When I left for studies you were just a seminarian. Now you're a priest. You look very much like your father. You remind me of him. How is he?" He answered, "Father, my father has been dead for almost three years now." We were both embarrassed. We realized we no longer belonged to the same community. He was not able to share a significant life experience such as his father's death with me, nor was I able to share his loss. You know that you are not a community member when you do not receive a *sharing of experiences*, and you are not allowed to enter the experiences of others. When you do not share common memories with others, you belong to different communities. Do poor and rich, powerless and weak, man and woman try to find a common field of experience? A community is born when there is a welcoming of my experiences by others and a welcoming of others' experiences into my own, resulting in shared memory.

From a common field of experience we move to the second degree, that of common and complementary understanding, which is also difficult to attain. It can happen that we have the same experiences and always understand our experiences in the same way. However, such is not always the case. We do not automatically move from experiences toward common understanding because the interpretations of our experiences are not always compatible. There are times when we outright disagree with one another. Mutual incomprehension is possible and breaks a community apart. In the extreme case, some people are "martyred" for the way they see and understand particular things. Reaching *common understanding* is made possible only by a process of dialogue, listening, and self-emptying, for which not everyone is prepared.

Lonergan identifies the third degree as the move to *common judgment* where we are able to affirm and deny the same things. If we affirm what others deny and deny what others hold true, then the event of community does not occur. That is one thing I admire about the Jesuits. After living with them for nine years, I know how much they differ from one another. But when they begin talking about the Spiritual Exercises, they affirm basically the same things. I am very happy that their source of community is their common affirmation of the Spiritual Exercises of St. Ignatius.

With common judgment, the search for community moves on to achieving *common decisions, commitments, and actions*, which requires a real investment among the individuals in the group. This degree of common meaning is manifested in dedication, loyalty and love, or faith for communities inspired by religion. We know the sense of being a community is slipping away from a family when the commitment of love wanes. A nation ceases to be a community when loyalty to fundamental societal values is gone. A parish is no longer a community when dedication to faith commitments dies.

What sustains the movement from one degree to another is communication. We cannot move from common experience to understanding, judgment, action, and commitment without the motor of communication. Unfortunately, the sophisticated means of communication we have achieved today as a hallmark of the global society has not translated itself into true communication. The only thing we have accomplished is the fast exchange of messages and information, but speed has little to do with true communication; communication goes far beyond the exchanging of information. Communication is present with the initial gift of a caring and nurturing presence that each individual in the group gives to the others. It is the Eucharistic presence, "This is my Body. This is my Blood. For you!" When we communicate, we hope we communicate with words the gift of ourselves, thereby giving birth to a community.

We cannot avoid having our hands dirtied in the task of forming a truly human community. It is this community that will make the entire world experience the power of the Eucharist. Theologian Karl Rahner calls the Eucharist the worship of the world that has been graced by God so that this world will live as one human family, as one human community where there is sharing, justice, and love. The church is the shining example of what is supposed to happen in the world. Through the Eucharist the church nourishes its own mission to celebrate, in the name of the world, the true worship of the One who gave his own self. The Eucharist keeps the memory of the crucified yet risen Lord alive as a common memory of the community that believes and hopes in him. It is in a true Eucharistic community that the world will recognize the Risen Christ, as happened to the two disciples on the road to Emmaus. Whenever we celebrate the Eucharist, we renew the reality of Easter in our lives.

The Appearance of Jesus to the Disciples

That same day, two of them were going to Emmaus, a village seven miles from Jerusalem, and they talked about what had happened. While they were talking and wondering, Jesus came up and walked with them, but their eyes were held and they did not recognize him. (Luke 24:13–15)

As they drew near the village they were heading for, Jesus made as if to go farther. But they prevailed upon him, "Stay with us, for night comes quickly. The day is now almost over." So he went in to stay with them. When they were at table, he took the bread, said a blessing, broke it and gave each a piece.

Then their eyes were opened, and they recognized him; but he vanished out of their sight. And they said to each other, "Were not our hearts filled with ardent yearning when he was talking to us on the road and explaining the Scriptures?"

They immediately set out and returned to Jerusalem. There they found the Eleven and their companions gathered together. They were greeted by these words: "Yes, it is true, the Lord is risen! He has appeared to Simon." Then the two told what had happened on the road and how Jesus made himself known when he broke bread with them. (Luke 24:28–35)

Another pivotal event that sets the direction for the coming Christian community as a sign of faith is the appearance of Jesus to the eleven disciples and their recognition of him. Jesus first appeared to the disciples where they were hidden in a locked room (John 20:19–25) and eight days later, again in a locked room, when Thomas was with them (John 20: 26–29), and finally when Peter and the disciples were fishing on Lake Tiberias (John 21:1–13). The Gospel of Luke also tells of the appearance of Jesus to Cleophas and an unnamed disciple on the road to Emmaus (Luke 24:13–32).

This short period between the death of Jesus on the cross and the realization that Jesus, indeed, was now the Risen One must have been a time of great frustration for the disciples. All of us have had experiences with frustration. We are frustrated with our economy, with peace and order, and even with the garbage. You are frustrated with your husbands and your children and your wives. When you are frustrated, you are on the road to Emmaus, just like the two disciples who were so filled with frustration they were close to despair. They hoped that Jesus would be the savior, the liberator of Israel, and then he was put to death. There were even rumors that the tomb was empty.

The daily experience of frustration is the beginning of an Emmaus experience—you are walking and someone joins you, someone who looks very ordinary, a stranger. Those of us reading the Gospel know that it is the Risen Lord, someone whose mystery of resurrection we cannot fully understand. But when he comes, he comes in a very ordinary manner. He visits us in very ordinary times, in times when we fall and just want to talk about it. He comes like someone who is ignorant and uninformed: "What is this one talking about?" When asked, you pour out your heart, "Why, it seems you are the only traveler in Jerusalem who does not know what has happened there these last days." The Risen Lord comes as a stranger, as someone who seems to be out of touch, who does not care about what has been happening in Jerusalem. He tells you, "How dull you are, how slow of understanding. You fail to believe the message of the prophets." The Risen Lord is really asking, "Do you really understand? Do you really know what is happening? Do you remember the messages of old?"

The situation has been reversed. The stranger who seemed ignorant now reveals the disciples' lack of understanding by going to the Scriptures. He opens to them, recalls for them Moses and the prophets, and explains all about himself. This stranger will open their minds and their hearts to the truth. The Risen One, though unrecognized, will explain to them who he really is. For it is not a biblical scholar, or a topnotch theologian, or a bishop who could best tell us about Jesus, but Jesus himself!

This stranger joins the two disciples at their house where he stays for the breaking of bread, a symbol of the shared life in one community. The breaking and sharing of bread is a domestic ritual among the Jewish people. The head of the family takes the bread, gives a blessing to God, praises God and in the very act of praising God, the bread is no longer ordinary bread but becomes a symbol of God's presence, of God's love. As the bread is broken and shared, the Risen Lord is recognized. The disciples realize, "It is the Lord." And then he disappears.

The beauty of the Emmaus experience is that is it very ordinary and very quiet. A seemingly ignorant stranger slowly leads the disciples to remembering, knowing, and understanding. Their bitterness and frustration, which used to numb their memories and understanding, turn into burning hearts. "Were not our hearts filled with ardent yearning when he was talking to us?" But the moment of recognition came only when they saw an act of sharing. They saw the Lord whose life and death were all about sharing—sharing his whole person, sharing his life, sharing his blood. He lived *for others*. It was an intercessory life, a life on behalf of the other. There was no moment when Jesus lived for himself, even the few times when he had to rest. When he saw the big crowd following, he would abandon his rest and continue teaching for they were like sheep without a shepherd. The disciples remembered, understood, and recognized this person for others at the breaking of bread.

It is significant that after they see and recognize the Risen Lord, he disappears. But now the disciples no longer need to see with their eyes. They have seen with their faith. They return to Jerusalem to tell the disciples there what had happened, that they have seen the Lord. The Risen Lord has written a new history for them—they move from ignorance to understanding, from forgetfulness to memory, from frustration to hearts burning, from going home to going to mission. The disciples' faith is rooted in their encounter with the Risen Lord in the Word and the breaking of bread. Each of us must ask himself or herself, "Is my proclamation rooted in an actual encounter with Jesus?"

All the research and preparation that we do to help us proclaim the Good News will be ineffective if our proclamation itself is not rooted in a real experience of and encounter with the Risen Lord. The true apostle and true apostolic faith acquire their true identity from this encounter. We again ask ourselves, "Is my prayer life a real encounter, a real living relationship with the Risen Christ? Is my encounter with the Word of God a transforming experience of the Risen Christ who teaches me again and again about himself?

Is our Eucharistic experience a re-birthing of the community of the Risen Christ? Does our faith in the Risen Christ lead us to share the experiences of sorrow and pain of others, to break the Word and bread to shed light on our common human condition and to form a community with the least of our brothers and sisters?"

Faith in the Risen Lord is his gift. He comes to us, appears and encounters us who have failed him with the offer of mercy and renewed communion. Faith is also our response of commitment to a new life with him as we remember him through the Word he speaks and the bread he breaks. Faith is the common field of experience, the source of common understanding and judgments, the common commitment of the Christian community. We now turn to the early Christian community to see how it lived by Easter faith.

2

The Path to Community

They were faithful to the teaching of the apostles, the common life of sharing, the breaking of bread and the prayers.

A holy fear came upon all the people, for many wonders and miraculous signs were done by the apostles. Now all the believers lived together and shared all their belongings. They would sell their property and all they had and distribute the proceeds to others according to the need. Each day they met together in the Temple area; they broke bread in their homes; they shared their food with great joy and simplicity of heart; they praised God and won the people's favor. And every day the Lord added to their number those who were being saved. (Acts 2:42–47)

The whole community of believers was one in heart and mind. No one claimed private ownership of any possessions, but rather they shared all things in common. With great power the apostles bore witnesses to the resurrection of the Lord Jesus, for all of them were living in an exceptional time of grace.

There was no needy person among them, for those who owned land or houses, sold them and brought the proceeds of the sale. And they laid it at the feet of the apostles who distributed it according to each one's need. This is what a certain Joseph did. He was a Levite from Cyprus, whom the apostles called Barnabas, meaning "The encouraging one." He sold a field which he owned and handed the money to the apostles. (Acts 4:32–37)

How did the life of the early church, the community of believers in Christ, develop? In the Acts of the Apostles, the humble life of the community focused on the relationship among the believers themselves (Acts 2:42–47) and between the believers and those outside the community (Acts 4:32–37). From these two accounts we will see the work of the Spirit, its power and presence in the faith that makes community life happen. We will also see that the life of the community is centered on communion, prayer, the Eucharistic table, and fidelity to the memory and faith understanding of who Jesus is.

The word "communion" is from the Greek word *koinonia*, whose root word is *koinos*, meaning common. One mark of the relationship among the believers is a deep sense of having something in common. The basic thing that makes them one community is their common faith in the Risen Lord. Thus the conviction of holding something in common comes from an interior spirit, a faith-inspired disposition that binds people together. This internal disposition expresses itself externally in community life. All attempts to fix whatever is wrong with community life are useless if they don't attempt to address its interior spirit at the same time. There is no authentic community without communion as its life force. There will be no exterior community without the internal spirit of *koinonia*. Communion is the heart of the Christian community and of every group of people, even non-Christians, who desire to become a community. It is from this heart that we determine whether a community exists. Where there is communion, there is purity in the heart of a community.

Sharing

The early church showed this spirit of communion concretely by the voluntary sharing of goods. The sharing of goods signifies commitment to one another. I remember one of my professors telling our class that when he was still a young seminarian in a religious community, he was given, as a gift, US$20. He thought of using it to buy a book. He went to his superior and told him about the gift and asked permission if he could buy a book using it. The superior said, "No. It does not work that way in community." My professor gave the $20 and his superior took it with his right hand. With his left hand, the superior took the same $20 and gave it to my professor saying, "There. You may buy the book," adding, "I want you to learn a lesson about community life. It is not because you have this amount and you are sure you will receive permission to use it that you can do so without first turning it over to the community. The community will permit you to buy the book." Some might think that that "ritual" is a waste of time, but it is a lesson about communion and community, expressed in holding goods in common so that they can be shared with one another.

The sharing of goods shows commitment to one another that results in not having even one needy or impoverished person in the community. Such a commitment leads to a decent quality of life, one lived inclusively and equally among each other. In an account that follows the reading above about Barnabas, Ananias and Sapphira died because they hid some of the proceeds of the sale of their land (Acts 5:1–11). This is how the early church described what happened to those who withheld from the community. To violate this free and voluntary sharing of goods was to sin against the purity of the Christian community, resulting in death.

The community did not just share goods; its members also shared their faith. In fact, their shared faith creates the inner disposition for sharing their goods with one another. They shared the Word of God and their most intimate experiences of God. This sharing is evident in the letters of St. Paul, who opened his heart to communicate his deep experiences of faith with his readers. It is truly a mystery that believers experience in distinctive ways the one faith in Christ. No one has a monopoly on encountering Christ. We need to share our story while receiving others' faith stories. When was the last time you shared with someone stories about how God has been forming and molding you as a Christian? Sharing our unique experiences of our common faith is part of *koinonia*, part of the work of the Spirit.

Elite globalization does not support a worldview of sharing. It thrives on acquiring and accumulating things for oneself or one's group, storing up goods even when others are in need of them. A community based on the sharing of goods, needs, and faith is a prophetic sign to a world divided by greed and selfishness.

Praying

The second aspect of the life of the community in the Acts of the Apostles is prayer. The early disciples retained the Jewish character of prayer, using the psalms, the prophets, and the teachings of Moses. The early disciples did not break their ties with the origins of their spiritual life that were rooted in the prayers of Israel. The prayer of Zachary, the canticle of Mary, and the song of Simeon do not mention Jesus but rather his ancestors Abraham, Isaac, and Jacob, whose hopes are now being fulfilled before their very eyes. We still use them as Christian prayers.

While the early disciples looked at how their ancestors in faith prayed, they also looked at how Jesus prayed. According to some biblical scholars who have studied the Lord's Prayer, what we are sure that Jesus did say are the words, "Our Father." I feel that what Jesus is trying to tell us is that it is not so much the formula but the experience of intimacy with God, of total trust and dependence on God, that counts. It is not so much the words but the heart that we bring and open up to God in prayer. Prayer is about experiencing communion with God, not just reciting fixed formulae. For Christians, communion with God in prayer and life is possible because we hold someone in common with God—Jesus, truly divine and truly human. Can I be intimate enough with God who is in heaven and call him *Abba*, as the Spirit of Jesus inspires us to do? Can I trust this God to provide my daily bread and protect me from evil the way Jesus abandoned himself to God? Prayer is a total experience. The prayer of Christians in the New Testament manifests their desire to be part of Jesus' very intimate experience of communion with God, to also draw close to *Abba*.

Prayer among the first Christians also expressed their expectation of Christ's return. *Maranatha!* Come, Lord! They wanted Christ to come soon; they wanted to have this union with Jesus again. They begged him to usher in the fullness of communion that we could not yet see because of sin, destruction and division in the world. Part of their anticipation was prayerfully recalling what Jesus said and did, and so with urgency they pleaded for him not to delay. The second coming of Christ has been so associated with fearful images that many people today seem to have abandoned this hopeful expectation. It seems that there is no longer this intense longing for Christ to come. But the early church's prayer was an act of remembrance, praise, and anticipation. In their prayer, past, present, and future blended into one.

It is also evident in the New Testament that prayer is first and foremost prayer for each other, for one another. According to Gerhard Lohfink, the reciprocal pronoun "one another" (*allēlōn*) that appears frequently in the epistles of the New Testament expresses the sense of community in the early church. They greeted one another, comforted one another, and prayed for one another. This prayer is another expression of *koinonia*. In the letters of St. Paul the various aspects of relationship in community, especially prayer, must take people as they are, respecting the uniqueness and needs of the individual persons. Community is about persons with faces and histories. Community is about human beings weaving their lives together in common dependence on God.

One of the features of elite globalization is the elimination of unique faces and histories of persons, societies, and cultures. Its success depends on hardness of heart, on not having to feel for "one another." Compassion might reduce my relentless drive for self-interest and profit. A community that always sees the faces of its ancestors and of neighbors will also see the face of God. That type of community will provide hope to a face-less world.

Breaking of Bread

A third aspect of community life among the early Christians was the breaking of bread, a term used for the Eucharist. The early disciples were a Eucharistic community, that is, they gathered together to break bread and to recall the passion and death of Jesus Christ until he came again. The breaking of bread during a meal is symbolic of the gathering of a people as a family in the sharing of life. St. Paul writes, "For as often as you eat this bread and drink the cup you proclaim the Lord's death until he comes" (1 Cor. 11:26). The breaking of bread reminds us of the broken body of the Lord, our Passover. In the Eucharistic prayer, the priest says, "Do this in memory of me." The Eucharistic celebration is a remembrance, a remembering made possible by the Holy Spirit. It is significant that before the narration of Jesus' actions and words at the Supper, before we remember, the priest says, "Let your Spirit come upon these gifts." The gift of the Spirit is needed in order to remember. Jesus himself said that the Spirit would remind his disciples of all that he had taught (John 14:26). The early disciples opened themselves to the power of the Spirit so as not to forget the life, death, and resurrection of the Lord.

By the breaking of bread we also express anticipation for Christ's coming in glory. It manifested the early disciples' longing for the return of Jesus and the beginning of the eternal banquet when heavenly food and wine shall be served. When that day comes, there will be no poor or rich; everybody will share the same food. The Dead Sea community broke bread with one of the seats around the table always left unoccupied in the hope that the Messiah would come as they broke bread. What about us? Is the Mass truly a symbolic expression of our yearning for the return of the Lord and the final transformation of the world? Every Eucharistic celebration should move the community to ask for this eternal banquet to become a reality in the present moment.

The closest experience I had to the early disciples' breaking of bread was eating with the *lumads*, the indigenous peoples of Mindanao in the southern part of the Philippines. I went to Mindanao to visit some seminarians sent to the place of the *lumads* as part of their pastoral immersion. At the end of the program, they had a thanksgiving and farewell party at the same time. During the meal, which was served on a buffet table, the *lumads* were put at the head of the line while the rest of us fell behind them. After a few minutes of conversation, we noticed that the line was not moving. The *lumads* had seated themselves around the buffet table of food and started to eat.

A sister who was a *lumad* herself went to ask them in their local language to get their plates of food and move to the empty tables so the others could serve themselves. We could see the embarrassment on their faces as they moved away from the table. We asked the sister what had happened. She explained that the *lumads* do not have a concept of an empty table. A meal is eaten around the table where there is food. While our basic unit of a meal is the individual plate, theirs is the common table, where the community is gathered and grows in the sharing of food and stories of life. They saw the table with food, gathered around it, and ate right there. After she explained it to us, I realized that we had just driven them away from their table. We had scattered them.

I felt sorry not so much for the *lumads* as for myself. I had been teaching about sacraments for many years and it was only then that I understood the symbolism of the breaking of bread. Perhaps we should recover the sense of "table" as a unit of our meals and promote the table of the Lord. We venerate the table as we begin the celebration of the Eucharist, the table around and on which we share one bread and one cup of blessing. The table is a symbol of the Lord who forms a community by hosting a supper for those whom he calls his friends. The early Christians are close to our indigenous brothers and sisters in this wonderful insight and practice.

The earth is like a common table for all to gather around and share life. But nowadays, the earth is claimed by those who wield power as their domain, to which those not of their kind are not invited to come near. The earth is destroyed in its purpose. The human family is impoverished because it cannot gather around the common table of the earth's bounty. A community that gathers to break bread gives hope to the poor grown weary of being sent away and waiting for crumbs to fall from the table of the rich who "own" the earth.

Desiring to Learn

Members of the early Christian community also opened themselves to the instructions of the apostles. The apostles were eyewitnesses to Jesus Christ. They were the ones who remembered most about Jesus and told and re-told his story. Aside from keeping his memory alive, the apostles also tried to interpret how Jesus would have dealt with the new situations of their time. Their memory and creative insight into who Jesus was and how he would have addressed certain situations were their contributions to the growing Christian community.

Learning is essential to building community. Every family, city, nation, or religious group is knit together by common stories and memories. But we have to learn them, listen to them, and make them our own in order to become a living part of that community. Someone who refuses to learn from the community's wisdom refuses to be part of that community. Even original thinkers and inventors depend on the knowledge of people before them. Learning is always a communitarian enterprise. As I child I learned about our family values through the stories our grandparents, great grandparents, and other relatives repeated to us, especially during All Saints' Day when we gathered around their resting places. Through those learning moments, I became more a part of the family. In the same way novices are initiated into religious communities by learning the life and spiritual wisdom of those who started the order.

A community grows stronger when learning becomes mutual. We are all ignorant; we need to learn from others. We all possess some wisdom; we must be generous in sharing it. A Christian community is one where the desire to know Jesus is great, where there is openness to his teachings and ways. At the same time, there is an eagerness to share what one has known of Jesus, growing insights into his mystery. The model is Jesus who taught with penetrating insight what he first heard and learned from Abba. The teacher is a learner.

Elite globalization has produced growth that cuts many people from the roots of their cultures and traditional wisdoms. Learning is a one-way process where those in a dominant position pretend they have nothing to learn from others. They only dictate. The global community is impoverished because precious lessons of hope from the poor, the victims, and the forgotten of this world are not heard.

Healing in the Spirit

Another mark of the early church was healing in the power of the Spirit. In Acts 3:1–26, Peter says to the crippled man, "I have neither silver nor gold, but what I have I give you: In the name of Jesus of Nazareth, the Messiah, walk!" (3.6). This account reveals a deep consciousness on the part of the early church that the good things they did were accomplished in the power of the name of Jesus. All the good works the apostles did could not be attributed to them alone. It was the work of the Spirit who gave them access to the powerful name of Jesus.

The Spirit allows us to participate in the power of the name of Jesus Christ. When the Spirit works, we are made aware that we do not and cannot do good things out of our own power. The Spirit leads us to a deep awareness of our lack of self-sufficiency and of our total dependence on the power of Jesus. Some people ask, "Why do we have to confess our sins to you, Father? How can a sinner absolve sins?" As a priest, I do not absolve in my name but in the name of the Father, and of the Son, and of the Holy Spirit. During the consecration at Mass the power of the Spirit is called upon, "Let your Spirit come upon these gifts to make them holy, so that they may become for us the body and blood of our Lord Jesus Christ."

This humble opening to the power of the name of Christ bore fruit in the form of healing. But the healing that took place was not just the restoration of physical health. Healing in the Bible is also the restoration of communion. Sickness isolates us from community and when we are healed we are brought back into the community. When Jesus healed, he restored; he gave the cured person back to the community. Jesus' very attention to the sick was the beginning of healing. He made the sick who were separated from the community or declared unclean know that they mattered. His disciples experienced how, through the Spirit, the name of Jesus made persons whole and also made communities complete.

How did the Sanhedrin, the council of leaders, respond to the bold proclamation and healing miracles of the apostles? In Acts 4:1–31 we see the beginnings of the persecution that would be experienced by the early church. The apostles preached the Good News and performed good deeds that stirred up anger within the priests, the Sadducees, and religious leaders. Peter and John were both arrested and forbidden to proclaim the name of Jesus. The power of the Spirit manifested itself in Peter and John and they continued to proclaim despite the Sanhedrin's stern warning. "Judge for yourselves whether it is right in God's eyes for us to obey you rather than God. We cannot stop speaking about what we have seen and heard" (4:19–20). The power of Jesus' name bursts through threats that want to stifle it.

When Peter and John were released and returned to the community, they spoke of the good news of their suffering for the sake of Jesus Christ. The Spirit enabled them so much that they rejoiced in their suffering for it was on account of the name of Jesus. The Spirit is the power to proclaim and preach in the name of Jesus Christ in the midst of antagonism and persecution. The Spirit whom Jesus surrendered on the cross with his last breath now breathes on the apostles to carry their crosses for Jesus.

There is no doubt that the world needs healing. The senseless death of countless people, especially of children, shows how wounded our world is. Even nature is severely injured. Whether death is inflicted by guns or unpaid debt, by embargo or persecution, it is misused and abused power that destroys. Power used to dominate or coerce does not give life. The early church relied on the power of the name of Jesus crucified, folly to the world but the wisdom of God. The name of Jesus heals because he bore all wounds rather than wounding others. His love is the power that unites people into community.

Gathering Together

One additional mark of community is gathering together. "They spent much time together," according to the Acts of the Apostles. This is a wonderful description of the church—those who spend much time together. The Greek word *ekklēsia*, the origin of *iglesia*, *l'église* or church, connotes a people called to come together. It begins with a call. The gathering is a response to the one calling. No one is called alone; it is always with others (con-vocation). In a real sense, the gathering does not stop even when the people have returned to their homes. They remain together in their common response called faith.

As a gathered community, no one should be made to feel alone, isolated, or neglected. One sign of the power of the name of Jesus is the deep sense of belonging that it instills among his followers. The good will toward neighbor manifested in the gathering of the early church in turn won for the disciples the good will of many people, and they grew in number (Acts 2:47). Gathering together as brothers and sisters is one of the most powerful ways of proclaiming the name of Jesus. At a time when many people feel lonely and abandoned, the church should witness to togetherness.

One way to understand this is my own experience of a fellow seminarian during my seminary years. He was extremely affirming of anyone who did well in an examination or simply finished a task. But his effusive appreciation looked artificial to me, as though he were overdoing it. So I took the courage to tell him that while we were grateful for his positive attitude, we also found it exaggerated.

He thanked me for the feedback. But he asked me, "Have you experienced being so happy about something you have done well but there is no one who shares your joy?" Then he recounted how his parents separated when he was eight years old. Since that day neither of his parents ever attended any of his school functions for fear of encountering the other. Being a consistent honor student from grade school through philosophy, he received medals at the end of every academic year but always without his parents to witness it and to share his joy. "I graduated *magna cum laude* in philosophy," he narrated. "My name was the last to be called. When I reached the stage I stood in front of the people waiting for a parent to pin the medal on me. But no one came up. I sobbed uncontrollably before the applauding crowd. I have never felt so alone. Then one of my professors came up the stage, played the role of my parent, proudly presented the medal to me and hugged me as her real son." I was stunned. Then he continued, "Now you know why

I am excessive in praise of others. I do not want any person to feel alone. Assuring people that I am with them is my way of getting healed too." In my heart I quietly thanked God that this person who suffered from abandonment but has experienced acceptance now gathers people together.

Isolation wounds. Togetherness heals. Looking at how scarred our people are, I wonder whether we are really isolating one another instead of becoming a global community. A Christian community is called to be a sign of a people who could be together, sharing common concerns and dreams, common pains and sorrows, and a common quest for life. Gathering together is our response to Jesus' cry on the cross that continues to echo in our time, "My God, my God, why have you abandoned me?" Let us put an end to isolating people; let us make others experience God in their lives by coming close to them in togetherness.

Sharing, praying, breaking of bread, desiring to learn, healing in the Spirit, and gathering together—these are simple actions that made and will continue to make the church a powerful symbol of community to a divided world.

3

A Community of Love

Now, on the first day after the Sabbath, Mary of Magdala came to the tomb early in the morning, while it was still dark and she saw that the stone blocking the tomb had been moved away. She ran to Peter and the other disciple whom Jesus loved. And she said to them, "They have taken the Lord out of the tomb and we don't know where they have laid him."

Peter then set out with the other disciple to go to the tomb. They ran together but the other disciple outran Peter and reached the tomb first. He bent down and saw the linen cloths lying flat, but he did not enter.

Then Simon Peter came following him and entered the tomb; he, too, saw the linen cloths lying flat. The napkin, which had been around his head, was not lying flat like the other linen cloths but lay rolled up in its place. Then the other disciple who had reached the tomb first also went in; he saw and believed. Scripture clearly said that he must rise from the dead, but they had not yet understood that. (John 20:1–9)

he life of the early Christians shows how faith in the Risen Lord can transform diverse persons into a community. The Christian community is not only a fruit of the resurrection. It has a mission to embody the new life that the Risen Lord offers to humanity and creation. Seeing our life as community, people may hopefully see none other than Jesus as the cause of our being together.

Is the Risen Jesus truly seen in the faith we try to live out every day? What elements contribute to our faith in Jesus the Risen One and our encounters with him? What factors affect our faith in Jesus? The twentieth chapter of the Gospel of St. John presents a number of different factors that affect belief in Jesus Christ, the Risen One. Many of these factors can be included in the metaphor of seeing.

Who has seen the Lord? How do they see the Risen Lord? Has any of us seen the Lord? In our ordinary language, seeing, believing, and understanding are intertwined. Often, when we see a puzzled look on someone's face, we ask, "Do you see what I mean?" We use the metaphor of seeing to indicate understanding. Remember Tevye, the father in *Fiddler on the Roof*, when he asked his wife, Golde, "Do you love me?" And she answered, "After all these years of cooking, of washing . . . you ask me? Have you not seen?" Perhaps we should ask ourselves, "Have I seen the Lord? And do people see that the Lord is truly risen in me?"

According to the Gospel of John, the beloved disciple saw the empty tomb and the burial cloths and he believed. Peter saw the same things, but John does not say whether he believed. For John the evangelist, Peter, who would play a prominent role in the early Christian community, was not the first one reported to have come to believe in the resurrection. The evangelist knew of someone called "the beloved disciple" who believed even before any appearance of the Risen Christ. He already "saw" even without a manifestation of the Lord. But how did this beloved disciple come to believe? Throughout John's Gospel, the beloved disciple is the image of the ideal follower, the one whom Jesus loved and the one who loved Jesus. Therefore the disciple who believed first was "the one who loved." His was a belief arising from *love*, not from an appearance of the Risen Lord. In love, this disciple did not need any other sign. Love had heightened his sensitivity to see. As far as the beloved disciple in the Gospel of John is concerned, love is not blind.

The one who loves sees what others do not see. Love opens what William Johnston calls the inner eye or a third eye—the eye of the heart, the eye of love. Only with love can the third eye see. This is true for all of us. When love is alive in us, we see more than what "non-lovers" see. Before their children can complain about anything, parents already see that something is going on. Some women do not need any evidence to know that their husbands are unfaithful because their long-suffering love sees what is happening in their marriage. Love heightens our capabilities and sensibilities, allowing us to see beyond what is before us as signs and truths.

What St. Paul wrote to the Corinthians about love is verified in John's Gospel, "it bears all things, believes all things, hopes all things, endures all things" (1 Cor. 13:7). When there is love, we believe. It is not always true that we need to believe first before we can love. Sometimes, it is the other way around—because of love, our belief deepens. The beloved disciple shows us that faith in the Risen Christ is as much a response of love as it is a product of an encounter with the Risen Christ. Who will see the Risen Christ? The one who loves Christ. To profess "The Lord is risen" is not merely to recite a formula of faith but is also a confession of love. It is the cry of a lover—the one who loves Christ.

The philosopher Gabriel Marcel said something like this, "When you profess love to someone, what you are saying is, 'I do not want you to die.'" When someone is in love, part of that love is a desire to make the loved one live forever. That is why even when a loved one dies, love impels us to hope that he or she is not truly dead. In my love my loved one always lives. Death can end life but not love, for true love is stronger than death. In the face of the death of a loved one, those who love make sure that the beloved will not fully die. In my heart, you will continue living. You will not totally die! From the perspective of the Gospel, we see the resurrection as an event of love. And so we ask ourselves, "Is the Risen Jesus truly seen in my love? Do I encounter the Risen Christ in my love?" Not only is the Easter season the time to love, it is also the time to purify ourselves in our loving, our incapacity to love, and our infidelities to the call of love.

> *On the evening of that day, the first day after the sabbath, the doors were locked where the disciples were, because of their fear of the Jews, but Jesus came and stood in their midst. He said to them, "Peace be with you"; then he showed them his hands and his side. The disciples kept looking at the Lord and were full of joy.*
>
> *Again Jesus said to them, "Peace be with you. As the Father has sent me, so I send you." After saying this he breathed on them and said to them, "Receive the Holy Spirit; for those whose sins you forgive, they are forgiven; for those whose sins you retain, they are retained."* (John 20:19–23)

The beloved disciple was the first to believe because he loved. Yet he was not the first to proclaim the resurrection. Mary Magdalene was the first to proclaim the Risen One to the disciples. How did the disciples react to her good news? Apparently, the disciples did not believe because they were still hiding in fear of the Jews. Had they believed, the disciples would have been at peace and celebrated with great joy. The disciples believed only when Jesus appeared to them and showed them his hands and feet. The disciples had to see him and then they believed what they saw. They had a different manner of reaching faith; it was simply their way: They had to see.

The Risen Lord greeted them the first day after the Sabbath when they gathered in the upper room with the greeting of a resurrection people, "Peace be with you." According to Scripture scholar Raymond Brown, the greeting of Jesus is not a wish. Instead it is a statement of fact and its translation should not be, "Peace be with you," as if peace was not yet with them. Peace is already with the disciples, as Jesus promised when he said, "Peace is my farewell to you." And so the more appropriate translation should be "Peace to you." Peace comes with the resurrection and accompanies those who are sent to proclaim the Risen Lord. Peace is the opposite not of war or violence but of fear. If we try to see the root of violence in the world, we find that it comes from fear—fear of losing power, domination, riches, a good reputation, influence, or comfort. The Risen Lord brings peace that wipes away all that fear. It is a peace that comes with the Spirit of forgiveness and reconciliation. Defenses and walls are not needed. We have nothing to protect and hide. We can begin anew from Christ who offered his life for us. If Jesus could die for us, what do we have to fear? If Jesus triumphed over death, of what use is fear? Peace comes when we are assured we have someone we can trust and depend on. "Peace be to you" also means "I am among you as someone you can trust. Have no fear."

The peace the Risen Lord brings often seems to be far from our day-to-day experiences. We see in the history of nations and of the world why peace is not attained. Like the disciples, we seem to be enveloped in fear much of the time. We do not know whom to trust, so we protect our lives, property, and interests against threats, real or imagined. The minute someone gets on the *jeepney*, a Filipino variation of the American military jeep that is used as a minibus, that person is not at peace. From one moment to the next that individual is trying to feel if his or her wallet or keys are still in his or her pocket. Early one morning my aunt woke up because she sensed something was wrong. She heard voices and there were people in our house—burglars. She decided to make noise so that they would know that someone was awake. When the intruders heard her, they ran away. But they brought fear to our house and that fear resulted in bars being put up surrounding the house to keep intruders from entering. There are so many bars now that it is difficult to get out of the house quickly! The world is so fearful of terrorism that travelers to other countries are presumed potential terrorists unless proven otherwise! The world lacks peace because nations do not trust one another. When trust fails, fear sets in and peace is gone.

Fear also prevents us from helping others. One time a Filipino nun, her American friend, and I were walking in New York City. It was evening time and we saw a man lying on the street who seemed to be near death. The American, who was a nurse, instinctively went down on her knees to help him. Passers-by tried to stop her, saying, "Do not touch him. If he dies, you'll be sued." She identified herself as a nurse and said that she could help the man. "No! Do not help," they insisted. It is ironic that someone who wants to help can be told not to help. Even generosity is now confronted with fear. Those who want to help others cannot trust that their good actions will be appreciated.

How do we celebrate the resurrection and the peace brought by the Risen Christ? In some mysterious way, people who live in the midst of darkness, fear, and death are the ones who are full of resurrection stories because it is to them the Risen Christ comes with predilection. Their misery has taught them not to trust institutions. But they know a truly trustworthy person when they see one. They see that in Jesus, crucified and victorious for them. Their stories of resurrection peace are stories of unwavering trust that casts out fear. We need to go to them, listen to their stories, and see the Risen Christ alive in them as someone they depend on. We need to feel the peace he brings by learning how to trust again in him rather than on things that give false security. It is important to be at peace, for it is this peace that must accompany the disciples of the Lord in their mission. With peace, the disciples can "Go."

> *After they had finished breakfast, Jesus said to Simon Peter, "Simon, son of John, do you love me more than these? He*

answered, "Yes, Lord, you know that I love you." And Jesus said, "Feed my lambs."

A second time Jesus said to him, "Simon, son of John, do you love me? And Peter answered, "Yes Lord, you know that I love you." Jesus said to him, "Look after my sheep." And a third time he said to him, "Simon, son of John, do you love me?"

Peter was saddened because Jesus asked him a third time, "Do you love me?" and he said, "Lord you know everything; you know that I love you."

Jesus then said, "Feed my sheep." (John 21:15–17)

In this account, Jesus directs his attention to Peter, who is asked three times over the same question, "Do you love me?" Most scripture scholars note that this serves as a contrast to Peter's triple denial: three times Peter denied Jesus so three times Peter confesses his love for Jesus. In this repentance experience, Peter replaces the history of denial with a history of love.

The first question Jesus asks is significant, "Do you love me more than these?" There are many interpretations as to what "these" refers to. Some interpret it as Jesus asking Peter if he loved Christ more than he loved the others. According to Raymond Brown, a better interpretation is that "these" refers to "other disciples." "Is your love for me more than the love of these other disciples for me?" It may sound like a competition existed among the community of disciples to see who loved Jesus the most. I maintain that this is, indeed, the stiffest kind of competition, but one that is allowable in our communities—who can love the most?

In chapter 15 of John's Gospel, Jesus says, "There in no greater love than this, to give one's life for one's friends" (John 15:13). When, in an earlier episode, Peter said to Jesus, "I will lay down my life for you" (John 13:37), he was saying, "I am the willing one in this group of disciples. I have the greatest love. You are my friend. I will prove it to you by laying down my life for you." At this moment before the passion of Jesus, Peter seems seized with a boldness that impels him to make a declaration without weighing the possible consequences. We know that Peter will fail and Jesus knew then that Peter would later deny him.

Yet now the Risen Christ asks Peter if his love for him is greater than the love of all the other disciples. Peter responds with a very different attitude, "Yes, Lord, you know that I love you." We sense that Peter has been chastised and humbled by his failure. Peter's presence by itself was a simple affirmation of love. Peter's confession of love is also an act of trust in Jesus' knowledge of Peter in that he responds, "You know that I love you," instead of a straightforward, "Yes, I love you." Peter trusts the Risen One who knows and accepts him better than he knows and accepts himself.

St. Paul echoes this trust in God in one of his letters, "I do not even judge myself . . . the Lord is the one who judges me" (1 Cor. 4:3–5). Peter's response tells us that even our most intimate act of love for Jesus Christ is something we cannot claim for ourselves as part of our own merit. Oftentimes, a *desire* to love Jesus is the best we can offer. Our act of love is thus an act of trust in Jesus who knows us. Should we fail in our fidelity to love Jesus, our love can also be an act of repentance to Jesus who knows us even before we fail. Before Peter's denial Jesus already said, "Satan has demanded to sift all of you like wheat, but I have prayed for you that your own faith may not fail; and you, when once you have turned back, strengthen your brothers" (Luke 22:31–32). Like Peter, we can all trust Jesus to continue loving us after our many denials of him. In fact, he envelopes us with his prayer even before we fail him. Although he cannot always depend on our love, we can always depend on his.

It is good to hear the Lord ask us, "Do you love me?" In response, we should do our utmost to express our desire to love God and to love Jesus, knowing that he is the Risen Lord who knows us from within because he is present to us from within. And our profession of this desire to love should be as humble as Peter's profession of love. Ours is not a profession of love from someone who has the world as witness to his or her fidelity, but it is an act of love that is grace, for Jesus knows our weak and at times inadequate human capacity to love. We should also be aware that this act of love does not end in a romantic relationship with Jesus but is instead enacted within our community.

In the Gospel of John, love is given primacy. After each profession of love, however, a corresponding mission is given to Peter. "Feed my lambs. Tend my sheep." Love and pastoral care go together. Love and outreach go hand in hand. Love, more than any other qualification, is needed for mission or any form of Christian care and service. St. Augustine, writing on this part of John's Gospel, says that shepherding is an *amoris officium*—the charge of love. For Augustine, the moment the human shepherds of our Christian communities lose love and are attracted to the powers, privileges, and prestige they acquire in the process of shepherding, they will no longer be able to care for the flock. They become the bad shepherds castigated by Ezekiel in the Old Testament (Ezek. 34:1–10). This serves as a reminder to the whole church, especially title-holders and office-holders within the church, about the primacy of love. When we who hold titles become beholden to the authority we possess, we should be reminded that what matters most is love, love for Jesus enacted in loving service of neighbors. Without love, service becomes power and authority becomes domination.

Jesus came as the Good Shepherd and he is the only Good Shepherd. When Jesus entrusts Peter with the mission, he says, "Feed *my* sheep." "Tend *my* lambs." They are neither *Peter's* sheep nor *his* lambs. The flock does not become Peter's property. "I know my sheep and my sheep know me." No one should have the nerve to think that he or she can be a substitute for Jesus the Good Shepherd. To do so is to go against the faith of the resurrection; it is to claim that the resurrection did not happen, that Jesus does not live and that the victory of the Good Shepherd is false.

Even bishops, priests, deacons, and other leaders of the church are not substitutes for the Good Shepherd; no one can take the place of Jesus the Christ. However, we *are* called to be symbols of Christ. There is a world of difference between being a substitute and being a symbol. A substitute is there because someone is absent. A substitute reminds us that someone is absent! Jesus is always present and because he is always present we do not need people to take his place. We do need people who will remind us in a living and effective manner that Jesus is present, that he is true, and that he is truly alive.

Shepherding in the Gospel of John is not a matter of lording it over others. Rather, the shepherd is expected to lead the sheep out to the pastures so they can eat. To be a shepherd means to know the sheep personally, to know them by name as the sheep know the shepherd by voice. And in the end, to be a shepherd is to lay down one's life for one's sheep. To be a shepherd is to lead, to love, and to die. We verify this in Jesus himself, the Good Shepherd. Jesus expected Peter to do likewise. He expects this of parents, teachers, government officials, religious figures, world leaders, peace advocates, environmentalists, and all with responsibilities for communities. They are all to be shepherds patterned after the Good Shepherd.

How then do those who have heard their names called by Jesus the Good Shepherd, professed their love for him, and received from him a share in his unique mission to be shepherds prevent themselves from ruling and lording it over others? If this happens, even though their intentions are good, they block the transparency of the presence and the work of the One Good Shepherd. Even though some of us have been called to feed the sheep and to tend the lambs, we should not forget that we are still part of the flock. Office-holders should never get so caught up in their identity as shepherds that they forget that they are still part of the sheepfold.

Every so often it is good for persons in positions of responsibility and leadership in the church, in society, and also in families to imagine themselves as sheep, and to look at how Jesus the Good Shepherd has been guiding them. By paying attention to how Jesus the Good Shepherd has been feeding us, we can learn how we can feed others in the way Jesus wants his sheep to be fed.

We began this chapter with a reflection on love that is stronger than death. Love also invites trust, casts out fear, and brings peace. We ended the chapter with a reflection on a love that is willing to die, like the love of Jesus, totally given to the sheep. No group of people can become a community without love. It is love stronger than death that enables the members to remain together in spite of faults and failures. It is love that builds trusting relationships that give peace to a community. It is love that transforms people into caring and self-sacrificing shepherds one to another in community. It is the love of the Risen Lord taking form in a community. This is what every Christian community should aspire to be.

The disillusionment brought about by neo-liberal and profit-driven globalization has caused so much distrust and fear in the world. People feed themselves with another's goods rather than feeding one another. Human beings are being sacrificed for profit rather than human beings making sacrifices for other people. The words of a song of yesteryears are appropriate for our time, "What the world needs now is love! It's the only thing that there's just too little of." A living Christian community can happen only when there is overflowing love. And that's what the world needs now!

4

A Community of Solidarity

But first he had instructed through the Holy Spirit the apostles he had chosen. . . .

When they had come together, they asked him, "Is it now that you will restore the Kingdom of Israel?" And he answered, "It is not for you to know the time and the steps which the Father has fixed by his own authority. But you will receive power when the Holy Spirit comes upon you; and you will be my witnesses in Jerusalem, throughout Judea and Samaria, even to the ends of the earth."

After Jesus said this, he was taken up before their eyes and a cloud hid him from their sight. While they were still looking up to heaven where he went, suddenly, two men dressed in white stood beside them and said, "Men of Galilee, why do you stand here looking up at the sky? This Jesus who has been taken from you into heaven, will return in the same way as you have seen him go there."

Then they returned to Jerusalem from the Mount called Olives, which is a fifteen-minute walk away. On entering the city they went to the room upstairs where they were staying. Present there were Peter, John, James and Andrew; Philip and Thomas, Bartholomew and Matthew, James, son of Alpheus; Simon the Zealot and Judas son of James. All of these together gave themselves to constant prayer. With them were some women and also Mary, the mother of Jesus, and his brothers. (Acts 1:2b–14)

Three separate episodes form this account: what happened before the Ascension, the Ascension itself, and the disciples gathering in an upper room. Together these episodes describe a movement toward the formation of a community, albeit a very unusual community. It is the Risen Lord who has initiated this movement. After Jesus' arrest and crucifixion, the disciples who had scattered were now gathered together by the Risen Lord. From the upper room they would go out to the whole world clothed with the power of the Spirit to witness to the resurrection.

It seems the disciples began to scatter even before the actual arrest of Jesus. Though their physical scattering occurred after the arrest, they had begun distancing themselves from Jesus and from each other. The bonds of communication weakened through time until they were eventually severed. One betrayed him, another denied knowing him, and all fell asleep in Gethsemane when asked to watch and pray. The promise of their initial calling was left unfulfilled, and the goals of discipleship were shattered. Friendships and promises to stay together were forgotten.

Only the Risen Lord could have gathered this wounded band again as one community. He started the process when he appeared to Mary Magdalene and the other Mary, instructing them to tell "his brothers" to meet him in Galilee (Matt. 28:1–10). For the disciples, Galilee was not just a place, it was also an event. It was in Galilee by the sea where they first saw the Lord. It was there where Jesus, as he passed by, saw Peter, Andrew, James, and John. It was there where their love story began, where first encounter and first love took place. It was also there where these fishermen left their nets, boats, and family to be with Jesus. It was an event of pure love and freedom, of building communion with Jesus. Sadly though, the events after the initial Galilee proved that the bonds of communion were precarious. Now, following their scattering, the Risen Lord wants to meet them again in Galilee where it all had begun.

It seems that this is the Risen Lord's way of offering a fresh start to his disciples. Jesus, the one who was hurt, the one who was made to feel that he was a failure, is surprisingly the one who offered to begin a new life with them. He has not lost hope. He calls them "brothers" and brings them together again. This gathering in Galilee is his act of hope that not everything has been lost. It is also the beginning of the community that gathered in the upper room, in the cenacle, to wait for the promised Holy Spirit.

The Galilee event happens in our lives too. As individuals and communities, we can recount our Galilees—those moments of innocent love, intense hope, and freedom. There may have been a moment in our life when we encountered Jesus vividly and perhaps later we "drifted away" from him and one another. But we always have the opportunity to return, and Jesus is waiting to meet us. Jesus is hopeful that we can start afresh. Jesus places so much hope in the goodness and capacity of human beings to be renewed, even though they have failed him and have strayed away from him time and again. It is Jesus who gathers them to be with him, brothers and sisters once more.

Jesus' offer of a fresh start is an act of forgiveness. Forgiving someone means freeing the offender from the shackles of sin and wrongdoing. It expresses hope that there is more to this person than faults and failures. At the same time, forgiveness frees the person forgiving from the possible prison of anger, hatred, and violence. It offers hope to the offended person, making him or her realize that there is more to his or her heart than harboring wounds. The cycle of evil begetting evil is broken by forgiveness. Offender and offended are brought in solidarity with each other in the act of forgiving. They both need liberation and a new life. Though they may seem to be worlds apart they really share the same human condition.

Galilee, an event of forgiveness, is an event of hope to all, a fresh start for all.

After returning to Galilee and gathering together again, the disciples rejoiced in the presence of the Risen Lord with them: "over a period of forty days he appeared to them and taught them concerning the kingdom of God" (Acts 1:3b). Here we see the story of discipleship beginning anew. But this instruction goes beyond what they learned initially. Jesus teaches them about the reign of God that is now personified in the presence of the Risen One. The reign of God is the triumph of compassion, forgiveness, and mercy. It is focused on Jesus' person, his life, his death, and his resurrection. A new community is being formed around the Risen One and it is necessary that Jesus teach them again about himself. Was it not Jesus who opened the eyes of the disciples on the road to Emmaus and made their hearts burn? By teaching them for a second time, Jesus prepares them for entering the upper room.

The community to be gathered in the upper room is more a community of learners than of teachers. They eagerly and ardently listen to Jesus' re-presentation or re-teaching of the reign of God to correct their previous misconceptions. A community of eager listeners and learners does not harbor the illusion that they have achieved full knowledge and that there is nothing more to learn. A true cenacle community is made up of people who are at peace with their incompleteness, and this incompleteness urges them to learn more from Jesus. It is a community where people say, "Because I am slow of heart to learn, so I am willing to be taught." The late Bishop Felix Paz Perez told us, "One of the worst things that can happen to you priests is to believe that you already know everything. If you refuse to learn, then you begin lording it over your parishioners. You will not allow lay participation and empowerment because there is no room for them in the mindset of a pastor who thinks he knows everything." He is right; such a person, especially a pastor, will encounter difficulties forming community.

An essential quality of the community in the upper room is a willingness to be taught. The offer of hope from the Risen Christ lies in our answers to the questions, "Can you learn again from me? Can you be taught again and again? Are you willing to be taught again?" These are questions of hope addressed to disciples of little faith or students who have fallen short but for whom the Risen Lord refuses to give up hope. But have the disciples given up on themselves?

When Jesus was eating with the disciples, he told them, "Do not leave Jerusalem but wait for the fulfillment of the Father's promise about which I have spoken to you" (Acts 1:4). This was an explicit command of the Risen Lord. After Jesus was lifted up to heaven (v. 9), his disciples returned to Jerusalem as he had commanded and entered the upper room. They apparently now knew how to listen to and follow Jesus' instructions! They could learn after all. There was hope.

Just like Galilee, Jerusalem is not just a place but also an event filled with significance. Jerusalem is associated with the Temple, including all the blessings and decay it connoted. It is the most fitting place for worship and also the best place for the corrupt practices of the chief priests and the Pharisees. It is a place of sacrifice and a place of commerce. Jerusalem is also the place where prophets are traditionally killed, a holy place that rejects holy people. Because of this, it is a severe test for authentic prophets. It is there where true prophets, such as Jesus, can emerge maligned and rejected on account of the truth to which they witness. All in all, Jerusalem is an ambivalent place, an event of ambiguity. Though wrapped in holiness, it is not immune to brokenness.

In Jesus' own life, "ambiguous Jerusalem" was a place of celebration. Every year his family went to Jerusalem for the festival of Passover, a remembering of Israel's liberation in the hope of final divine intervention. There the twelve-year-old boy separated himself from father and mother to be in his Father's house and to read scripture. Many times over, Jesus would return to Jerusalem until that last fateful entry to the welcome of "Hosannas!" befitting a true king and prophet. There in Jerusalem, in his Father's house, he would be sold and sacrificed as a political pawn. In Jerusalem he would suffer death, like so many other prophets. By bearing all the ambiguities of Jerusalem, Jesus became the New Jerusalem.

The Risen Lord now tells his disciples to remain in Jerusalem to wait for the promised Spirit. The Spirit will transform them into prophets and witnesses of Jesus, the prophet of the reign of God. It is in Jerusalem where they are to undergo what the prophets of old up to Jesus experienced—the confirmation of their mission to be prophets, witnesses, and friends of God. From Jerusalem, the disciples are to go to all nations. But they must remain in Jerusalem until the proper time. In "ambiguous Jerusalem," their ambiguous selves would be purified for the mission they have received from their teacher.

At the beginning of this chapter, we identified the dynamics of the formation of a community through the scattering of the disciples, the re-convocation of their community, their re-learning from Jesus, the ascension of Jesus, and their gathering together in the upper room. The Risen Lord initiated and followed this movement by offering the hope of a new community educated in the reign of God and transformed into witnesses. In other words, the cenacle community is a community of human beings transformed by Jesus and the Spirit. Sometimes when we speak of community our attention focuses solely on "What can *we* do? How can *we* blend personalities? Temperaments? Age groups? Culture? Language groups?" These are all valid concerns. But from the beginning until they gathered in the upper room, the disciples' community was the creation of Christ and the Spirit.

Had the Risen Christ not offered a second gathering, the disciples would have remained scattered. Had he not offered a second education, they would have been entrenched in misunderstandings about the reign of God. Had he not directed them to stay in Jerusalem for the coming of the Spirit, they would have wallowed in cowardice. Every community that wants to pattern itself after the one gathered in the room upstairs must allow Jesus to fashion it into a community of hope.

Do we want to be signs of hope in our community? How can we be the offer of Jesus' hope to our neighbor? We cannot be signs of hope by running away from our "ambiguous Jerusalems." We have to remain in Jerusalem and discover our true selves. We live ambiguous lives, and must admit it. We try our best to put our world in order, but must recognize our failure in achieving it. We can all identify with St. Paul who says, "What I do, I do not understand. For I do not do what I want, but I do what I hate" (Rom. 7:15). In his seeming helplessness, he cries out, "Miserable one that I am! Who will deliver me from this mortal body? Thanks be to God through Jesus Christ our Lord" (Rom. 7:24–25). To become signs of hope in our communities, we should allow the Risen Christ and his Spirit to work through us in the way they choose. If we just do it our way, nothing will happen, for it is sometimes easier to give up than to continue hoping in God. We must continually remember the hope of the Risen One who transfigures crushed human beings into heroic witnesses through the renewing Spirit.

The Need to Break Down Isolation

The path to community lies in solidarity. Solidarity comes through intentionally breaking down barriers between people so they can communicate with each other. We usually think of death as being biological, occurring when the body's organs and systems fail, but death is not just biological. Death is also the termination of communication. True death is experienced when the possibility of communion, the possibility of personhood, is no longer present. Personhood involves being able to communicate both with others and with God. When we are no longer able to do this, we are *truly* dead.

We do not have to die a physical death to be dead to life. Many people are already in the place of the dead because they isolate themselves and do not communicate. They may inhabit a beautiful mansion and yet live in Hades. When there is no full communion with one another in the same house and full communion with God, then we become the *living* dead. Many people seem to be already dead in this sense today. Even surrounded by people, they are alone if they have no one with whom they can share their sorrows and—even more difficult—their joys. And it seems that with the increasing fragmentation of the world today (even in this so-called global world that supposedly eliminates borders and brings us closer together), the number of dead people is increasing. The breakdown of communication isolates us from one another. We ignore people as though they were dead. Sometimes isolating others takes the form of actual infliction of death through violence and killing.

As a young priest, I was invited to bless the house of a family I did not know. The priest who was supposed to bless the house had an emergency and he had given my name to the family. Since it was an emergency I agreed, but I reminded them that I had another appointment. I would bless their house and then leave immediately. They said, "Good, good. It's okay, Father."

A car came to collect me. The family's three grown children came along, with one driving the car. No one greeted me. When they learned that I was Father Chito they just opened the door and I got into the car. From the seminary where I lived to the house, no one communicated with me. Of course, the driver had to mind his driving, but the two other siblings were not communicating with me because they were busy "texting." I said to myself, "Well, it's okay. If they don't want to talk to me then what can I do? I cannot impose myself." But I was feeling bad. Where was our traditional Filipino courtesy? *Magandang hapon man lang*, a "Good afternoon" would have sufficed. I wanted to remind them that they were inconveniencing me and I deserved some respect. Since I could not communicate my own frustration, it was rapidly building up.

What somehow calmed me to some degree was when I realized that these two young people were texting one another. They were there in the same car and they could not even talk with one another. One of them finally asked out loud, "Hey, what is this that you sent? I can't understand your text." Instead of explaining it, the other sibling said, "Oh, okay. I will send you another message."

How puzzled I was, thinking that perhaps the new name of Hades or the place of the dead is "cell phone." It has been said that the cell phone is a way of "bonding" or communicating. Really? Or does it produce more dead people? I doubt that we are really bonding in the sense of achieving the fullness of personhood where people can enter our hearts and we can share our hearts with others. This is what life is all about. Life means being in communion with others and with God. We feel fully alive when we experience solidarity with other people.

Solidarity means joining a particular community not because we are bringing strength that others do not have, not because we are bringing contributions from our bounty, and not even because we are bringing something the community lacks. Solidarity means that we go to others as someone who shares their condition of need. We bring our needs to their needs. We bring our weaknesses to their weaknesses. We bring our fear and trembling to their fear and trembling. We go as someone who experiences the loneliness and isolation of daily deaths that they also experience. We approach them not from a position of superiority but from communion in helplessness. Like Jesus who went into the place of the dead as one who has died, we break people's isolation by living in solidarity, not pretending to be more alive than others but admitting we are as dead as they are.

It seems that support is easier than solidarity. This world does not lack for support because it is relatively easy to do. We can send a check to any number of charitable causes or within less than a minute we can click with our "mouse" on the Internet and simply enter a credit card number. Then we simply continue on our own way. Or we can participate in a food drive by sending a box of instant noodles or some cans of tuna. However, our lives go on without significant changes. We may even benefit financially by getting a tax deduction. But this is not solidarity.

Stories can be very useful to explain or illustrate a mystery. The two stories below, both from my Filipino context, tell much of the mystery of solidarity and community and how this mystery can be lived by people.

In 1989 I lived in Rome with the Immaculate Heart of Mary Fathers while I was doing research. I was the only Filipino in a small community of eight student priests. At that time, the superior of the house was a Belgian who had been a missionary in the Philippines. He had a married cousin who was an executive in Rome. During one of his visits, the Belgian priest mentioned to his cousin that a Filipino priest was living with them. The cousin and his wife immediately invited the Filipino priest to join them for dinner. When I learned of the invitation, I told the Belgian priest, "I don't know your cousins. I might not enjoy the evening." I thought that a meal with strangers would be too uncomfortable so I declined the invitation. The priest replied, "But my cousin is insisting because their maid is Filipino and their driver is Filipino."

This explanation offended me at first. It was as if I was being invited so that they could show that they had a Filipino maid and a Filipino gardener (they were husband and wife). This did not sound good to my ears. However, because the Belgian priest, who was also my host in Rome, kept insisting, I agreed to join them for dinner.

True enough, when we arrived at the house, it was the Filipina dressed in a maid's uniform who greeted us at the door. I was introduced to her and when she found out that I was Filipino too—I look Chinese—she reacted in a typically Filipino way. "Father! How is our beloved country? From where are you in the Philippines?" I told her I was from Cavite. She and her husband were from the Visayas but grew up in Manila. She was eagerly trying to look for some kind of connection between us. I could feel her deep sense of isolation and now, suddenly, there was this chance contact.

She asked me about so many things and I answered however I could. I did not know her at all, but we continued exchanging stories. At that time I was still studying in the United States and knew a great deal about Washington, D.C., and the U.S. in general, but I had little idea of what was actually happening in the Philippines. It then struck me that I was also isolated. They were isolated and there I was, with them. The ones in isolation met. The dead went to the dead and an explosion of life resulted.

I learned that she had a master's degree in education and had taught in a university in Manila. Her husband had studied and taught criminology. Their two children both attended medical schools and they could not afford the fees on their teachers' salaries. She told me, "Father, every day we just forget about our degrees. When we start picking up the laundry or do the dishes, we just try to keep those things from our minds. I don't let it enter my mind that I might have received a higher education than my employer. I just think of my children." We kept exchanging stories and even shed tears together.

After several minutes, the executive's wife came out and said that dinner was ready. Her maid was surprised. "Oh, my! I was not able to help out in the kitchen!" She panicked, saying, "Father, just a few minutes. I have to rush to the kitchen." But the Belgian woman stopped her and told her to change her clothes. "No, tonight you will be my guests. Go to your room and get dressed." The Filipino couple protested. I said to them in Filipino, "Go ahead. Give in to their request. Change your clothes." They went to their rooms and came out wearing beautiful clothes that had obviously not been used for a long time. The woman had arranged her hair and put on make-up and her husband wore a *polo barong*. Their fine clothes showed the creases from having been packed away and the Filipino couple also looked somewhat uncomfortable in their formal clothing.

What a dinner it was! The maid and the driver sat with us priests while the Belgian couple served us dinner and entertained us. I could not eat for sheer joy. I do not even remember what kind of food was served. There was a real sense of liberation. The king and queen of the house became the maid and gardener. The former king and queen joined the ranks of the dead and started serving. It was hard to remember who was who at that dinner—who was the lord of the house, who was the maid, who was the priest? It was just one community of life and love. It was the gathering of the "dead," all foreigners in Italy, but breaking each other's isolation.

I am quite sure that everything was back to normal the following day. The lord of the house would still be the lord of the house, and the maid would still be the maid. However, I am sure that new life entered that family, a bit of difference, a bit of liberation, thanks to solidarity.

A second story also tells of the bond between people that leads to communion. I was still a student in Washington, D.C., when a Filipino woman friend who had lived in the United States for fifteen years decided to go home for Christmas. She was very excited and wrote to many friends and relatives about her upcoming vacation in the Philippines. Her friends and relatives were also excited about her visit, especially since it would be at Christmas. They wrote back but their letters always cautioned her about the rising crime rate and the lack of peace and order in Manila. She finally called me to say that she was having second thoughts about going home. I told her to go home but reminded her to be careful and not flaunt her U.S. dollars.

She arrived in Manila before Christmas overwhelmed by her fears. Everywhere she went she clutched her purse tightly to her chest in case someone might grab it. She constantly thought, "These children, these poor people on the streets, they're only out for one thing, out there to abuse. They're out there to steal. I'm the one who just came from the States. I'm the rich person they'll want to steal from." Her fear neatly split the place of the dead—the dirty, the poor, those in need—from her own, which she had to protect.

Just a few days before Christmas, she and her brother were driving along one of Manila's main thoroughfares when their car broke down. Her brother, who was driving, said, "I'll call a mechanic. Do you want to wait inside the car? We can lock you in or you can stay outside. We'll lock the car so that if anything happens you can just make a run for it." She said, "Okay, I'll wait outside."

Standing next to the car, she kept praying, "Lord, protect me from hold-uppers. Lord, protect me from beggars. Lord, don't send any children to me. Don't send any beggars to me." And she continued with "Lord, protect me from this" and "Lord, protect me from that." She asked the Lord for protection from everything she feared. But God sent a beggar, a little boy.

"Miss, we haven't had lunch yet. My mother said that you might be able to help us. Can you give us some money to buy food?" asked the boy. My friend panicked, opened her purse, and without looking, gave the first bill she took hold of—500 pesos (roughly the equivalent of US$9.00). When she saw it, she thought, "*Naku!* Five hundred!" but she gave it anyway. She did not give out of charity but out of fear, thinking, "I've given you something, now leave me alone. Don't bother me anymore. I'm just minding my own business."

Suddenly she thought, "That boy might tell other people that there's a woman giving away five hundred pesos in the street. More people might come asking me for money!" All kinds of thoughts entered her head. The boy might return and tell her that they did not have any food for dinner. She could not stop thinking about it and she felt more dread and fear by the minute.

The boy did return. He said, "Miss, my mother said the money you gave was too much. There is so much food. We would like you to eat with us. Please come now."

She answered, "I can't go with you. I am watching over the car."

"But we live just right there," said the boy, pointing to a shack near the road. It was like the other shacks along Roxas Boulevard, those that had plastic shopping bags for walls, the kind that most people pretend not see while they're out driving. "While we're eating, we can watch your car."

Something must have happened to my friend because she followed the boy. She went to the place of the dead, the home of those apart. She went into the shanty and saw the boy's mother, an infant, and three other small children. The first words of the mother to her were, "Miss, the money you gave was too much. Here is the change. I just really didn't know where to get food for my children. My husband hasn't gotten his salary yet. I'm so embarrassed but I didn't know what else to do because the little ones have to eat."

My friend then told her, "Go ahead. Keep the money. You might be able to use it for tonight or for tomorrow, for Christmas."

The mother invited my friend to eat with them and she joined them. She held the baby and played with the children. She told me afterward that she forgot all about her car. The setting must have cast a spell on her. She also told me that it was the best Christmas dinner she had during her vacation. It was the first time she had ever entered one of the shanties or held the hand of a poor woman. "That was the first time I was able to hold an infant born to a squatter's family," she said. Then she added, "They were wonderful, generous people."

She went to the place of the dead but she had to be willfully dead herself—dead to all of her pretensions and emotions. It was only then, when by a stroke of grace she forgot all about the car and what that car stood for, she was ready to enter the place of the dead. New life did spring forth. For her it was the best Christmas, the best meal. And I am confident that for that family it was also a kind of visitation, an experience of grace.

That is solidarity. True community is born when people are willing to break each other's isolation, to visit the places of the dead in order to restore communication and life. But it asks of us to come not as someone pretending to be the only one alive among graves of dry bones. The Crucified Lord visited the place of the dead as a signal that new life comes to them from one who shared their death. It edifies me no end to see the crossing of boundaries not of capital, labor, consumer goods, and materialistic lifestyles but of food for the hungry, advocacy for debt cancellation, defense of women and children, love for the earth, and action for peace. That is true globalization. No marginalization, only solidarity!

5

Praying Together

After Jesus said this, he was taken up before their eyes and a cloud hid him from their sight. While they were still looking up to heaven where he went, suddenly, two men dressed in white stood beside them and said, "Men of Galilee, why do you stand here looking up at the sky? This Jesus who has been taken from you into heaven, will return in the same way as you have seen him go there."

Then they [the disciples] returned to Jerusalem from the Mount called Olives, which is a fifteen-minute walk away. On entering the city they went to the room upstairs where they were staying. Present there were Peter, John, James and Andrew; Philip and Thomas, Bartholomew and Matthew, James, son of Alpheus; Simon the Zealot and Judas son of James. All of these together gave themselves to constant prayer. With them were some women and also Mary, the mother of Jesus, and his brothers. (Acts 1:9–14)

According to this account of the ascension in the Acts of the Apostles, the disciples stood gazing up, following Jesus with their eyes as he was taken up into heaven. They witnessed the ascension after having spent several days with the Risen One. When the two men asked them, "Why do you stand there?" they could really have meant, "Where have you been? What led you here? What have you been doing? What have you seen?" If we ask the disciples where they have been, they would point to a period in their lives when the Scriptures described them as people of little faith. They had experienced the passion and death of Jesus. The passion was a time of humiliation with the disciples hiding in fear and Peter denying Jesus. After this time of humiliation, uncertainty, and hopelessness came the beautiful resurrection encounters with the Risen Lord. When the merciful and compassionate Risen Lord spent time with his disciples who had forsaken him, they recognized him with eyes of faith and with eyes of love. Now they stood and witnessed Jesus rising to the skies.

Prayer in the Upper Room

After the ascension, the disciples went to Jerusalem, to the upper room to be together. The upper room—the cenacle—was a place where the disciples prayed. Perhaps it was not just a place of prayer but also an event of prayer. According to Acts 1:12–14, the disciples devoted themselves to constant prayer in the cenacle. What form did their prayer take? It was not a schedule, not a technique, not a structure, not an obligation, and not even a rule. Prayer in the cenacle was a living and loving relationship with God that went beyond the present moment. It was a "prayer-in-waiting" for the fulfillment of God's promise, the coming of the Holy Spirit.

What does it mean to wait in prayer? To wait means to be receptive, to be like beggars asking to receive whatever the other is willing to give. It is often difficult for us to wait because we are used to taking action, to being the givers. The receptivity present in the experience of waiting is difficult to achieve because it reminds us that we are not in control. As beggars we wait until the grace, the gift, is given, whenever the giver decides to give. As beggars we cannot determine the shape that the gift will assume. This gives us the freedom to receive and see God's love and bounty not only in health, in good times, and when the sailing is smooth, but also in sickness, darkness, and even turbulent waters.

Another element of waiting is humility. Humility is not passivity or not having a mind of our own. Humility, instead, is allowing God to be God. We might wrestle with God like Jacob but we have to allow God to be God. In humility, we must remain where we are until the promise is fulfilled. God determines the right time. To stay and wait is very difficult in this age when everyone seems to be in such a hurry and where motion and obsolescence are accepted modes of life.

Finally, waiting in the cenacle is to wait in hope. The disciples waited for a promise, the promise of the Holy Spirit who would fulfill what Jesus had begun. It was a waiting that looked to the fulfillment of a future. The many times we have waited in frustration and anger were experiences of despair, but in the cenacle, waiting was hopeful anticipation.

To wait in prayer then is to become receptive, humble people of hope. If we pray in utter receptivity and humility, staying in focus and in hope, then our prayer becomes a formative experience. We are formed into receptive persons, humble, persevering, and hopeful persons. The quality of a person's prayer becomes the quality of the person.

While the disciples waited in prayer in the upper room, they did not pray as individuals but together as a body. Part of the cenacle experience is the mystery of people praying as one heart, as one community. Through prayer, separate individuals are joined together. Sometimes when I preside over the Eucharist and the sacraments, I feel that the five hundred people gathered with me in the church are five hundred individuals who just happened to be in the same place at the same time. When I say "The Lord be with you" and they respond "And also with you," it seems as if each individual is responding with his or her isolated heart and not as one community. But special moments of cenacle do appear when the assembly prays, sings, and even dances as one heart, one voice, and one body.

The disciples gathered in the cenacle prayed *as* a community, and the community that gathered was quite revolutionary because men and women were both present. This was the birth of a new community centered on the Risen Lord. Prayer can bring forth a new community of equals, of full dignity between men and women. We have seen occasions of how prayer can bring together Christians of different traditions into an experience of community. The gathering of the leaders of the various religions of the world in Assisi to pray generated so much good will and hope.

While the disciples waited in prayer as one community, their prayer was joy-filled. The prayer event in the upper room included remembering their experiences with Jesus and trying to understand them more deeply, which brought them great joy. With the coming of the Spirit, the joy of their prayer would overflow into witnessing. Witnesses to the Risen Lord are true only to the extent that they themselves experienced the Good News. Our primary model for witnessing can be found in the first letter of John: "So we tell you what we have seen and heard, that you may be in fellowship with us, and us, with the Father and with his Son, Jesus Christ. And we write this that our joy may be complete" (1 John 1:3–4).

The disciples who entered the cenacle were not individuals who set out to proclaim ideas or concepts. The prayer of the disciples did not isolate them from life or their real experiences; after all, the center of their life was Jesus. By their prayer, they were able to cherish and deepen this life. The central proclamation of the community gathered in prayer in the upper room was their experience of Jesus—what they saw, heard, touched with their hands, and remembered with joy.

Prayer and the Fruit of the Spirit

Pray at all times as the Spirit inspires you. Keep watch, together with sustained prayer and supplication for all the holy ones. (Ephesians 6:18)

All those who walk in the Spirit of God are sons and daughters of God. Then, no more fear: you did not receive a spirit of slavery, but the Spirit that makes you sons and daughters and every time we cry, "Abba! [this is Dad!] Father!" the Spirit assures our spirit that we are sons and daughters of God. If we are children, we are heirs, too. Ours will be the inheritance of God and we will share it with Christ; for if we now suffer with him, we will also share Glory with him. (Romans 8:14–17)

We are weak, but the Spirit comes to help us. How to ask? And what shall we ask for? We do not know, but the Spirit intercedes for us without words as if with groans. And He who sees inner secrets know the desires of the Spirit, for he asks for the holy ones what is pleasing to God. (Romans 8:26–27)

God has revealed it to us, through this Spirit, because the Spirit probes everything, even the depth of God.
    Who but his own spirit knows the secrets of a person? Similarly, no one but the Spirit of God knows the secrets of God. We have not received the spirit of the world, but the Spirit who comes from God and, through him, we understand what God in his goodness has given us. (1 Corinthians 2:10–12)

In these passages Paul, in his letters to the Ephesians, Romans, and Corinthians, describes how prayer should function in the life of the early Christians. The texts stress that prayer happens only in the Spirit. While we may feel that *we* are the ones praying, it is truly the work of the Spirit who is in intimate union with us. The Spirit's union with us is so deep, profound, and complete that it is difficult to distinguish what the Spirit does and what we are doing. Such is the case in prayer. We go to God in prayer and we feel as if we have prayed; however, it is the Spirit who not only makes it possible for us to pray but also prays for us, with us, and in us.

    The text above from Paul's First Letter to the Corinthians

describes this work of the Spirit. The Spirit scrutinizes the depths of God and the depths of our hearts. No one knows what lies within the depths of God but the Spirit of God, and no one knows what lies within the depths of human hearts except the Spirit dwelling in our hearts. St. Augustine said, "You are more intimate to me than I am to myself." God, in the power of the Spirit, knows the depth of our hearts more than we ourselves.

Prayer is an occasion for the Spirit to reveal to us *new* depths, new in the sense that we are not always aware of what is happening in our hearts. If we look closely enough, we may discover that what is in the depths of our hearts is the Spirit—God indwelling—rather than pain, concern, or ambition. Prayer can bring this awareness to us. Because the Spirit is our deep union with God, the Spirit is our prayer. Our prayer then is not so much what we want to say to God as what the Spirit says to God for us. It is as simple as that and perhaps because of its simplicity, it can be difficult to understand unless it is lived and experienced.

In the third passage above, from Paul's letter to the Romans, Paul writes that we do not know how to pray as we should. We are able to pray because the Spirit intercedes with groans we ourselves cannot express. There, thanks to the Spirit in the depths of our hearts, we are able to express what we want to say. In some ways, it is not our problem when we find it difficult to pray. It is the Spirit's problem because *we* "do not know how to pray as we ought." Our part is to open some space in our hearts to give the Spirit the chance to bloom and freely intercede on our behalf. When we feel we have poured out our hearts to God in prayer, in the eyes of faith, we say that it is the Spirit who prayed for us. Then we begin to feel that our prayer is true, transparent, genuine, and effective. It is indeed our prayer but at the same time it is the Spirit interceding for us.

How does this happen? According to St. Paul, the Spirit makes us pray for what God wills, for what is pleasing to God. The Spirit arouses and instills in our hearts prayer that makes us one with the will of God. Through the Spirit, our prayer is obedience to and oneness with the will of God. Prayer with the Spirit working in our hearts is not so much getting what we want from God, but our moving closer to oneness with the will of God. True men and women of prayer say that prayer is the path to the simplicity of poverty, obedience, and chastity. These three interior movements are encapsulated in a life of prayer. Poverty is to not have my desires but the desire of God; obedience is not my will but God's will; and chastity is the purity of desiring only what the Spirit of God desires. Prayer in the Spirit is to live in and for God. It is to cry out, "*Abba*, Father!" as though it were our last and only cry.

Yves Congar, the great French Dominican who later became a cardinal, has written that there is a distinction between "prayed petitions" and "praying prayer." He maintains that it is "praying prayer" that is prayer in the Spirit. Prayed petitions that express our desires and our needs are not a bad idea. These are petitions articulated in the form of a prayer. We express our needs and desires to God because we feel impotent and powerless to accomplish them. We ask someone more powerful to accomplish our desires and fulfill our longings. Prayed petitions are really experiences of transcendence, of a certainty that someone greater than me listens and cares. They are also a profound experience of human limitation that does not necessarily lead to despair but to openness to mystery. So expressing these desires in prayed petition is not bad, but, in the end, we have to be aware that what might dominate is *my* desire and *my* need—things that *I* cannot accomplish by myself. God might become a commodity kept in a closet, brought out when needed but locked up after use. Congar says that in prayer some people consider God as a mere extension of my arm that is too short to reach what I want to reach. Or we could be so caught up in our needs that we become blind to others' needs. I pray for a good job, but do I pray for the many other unemployed people? I pray for the approval of a housing loan, but do I pray for the homeless?

On the other hand, "praying prayer" is praying to God for what God wills. A classic example is Jesus praying in the garden of Gethsemane. Jesus expressed his desire, "My Father, if it is possible, let this cup pass from me," but in the end, he says, "yet, not as I will, but as you will." Jesus' prayer of agony recognizes God as God, resulting in an eventual union with the will of God. In praying prayer, we express our desire but if it is not God's will then we pray let God's will be fulfilled. I consciously seek whatever pleases God.

If we pray with the Spirit in our hearts and allow the Spirit to intercede for us, then our prayer expresses the relationship of the divine persons in the Trinity. As Jesus centered his prayer, indeed his very life, on seeking and doing the Father's will, so the Spirit enables us to pray to the Father as did the Son. It is this form of prayer that allows us to be caught up in the divine conversation where the Spirit makes us cry out with the Son, "Father!" Like the Spirit-filled Jesus, we can also pray what is humanly difficult to say, "Not my will but your will be done."

There are times when prayer is the first to suffer because of our busy schedules. We rationalize that God will always understand and God is always there anyway. We have deadlines to meet and so we neglect our prayer life. But there will always be deadlines. Some priests and religious men and women say that a weakened prayer life has caused them to lose focus. Lay people declare even more openly the disharmony that enters their family life, work, relationships, and values when prayer is neglected. Unless we go to the depths of prayer in the Spirit, we will never see prayer as an indispensable part of our life. Only when we enter into "praying prayer" will the experience of a living relationship with God root itself in the depths of the heart and of the community.

Like many other Christians, we Filipinos have a special love for prayed petitions. With our petitions, we are humble and poor. Our popular expressions of faith and devotion convey this childlike longing to be heard by our Father. This is fertile ground for praying prayer. We Filipinos, like most Christians around the world, need to develop a true spirit of discernment that will lead us to scrutinize the depths of our hearts, culture, government, economy, political system, and religiosity so we can better conform them to the will of the Father. Only this form of prayer will shape lives of the justice and righteousness that bring about peace.

The Fruits of Praying Prayer

But the fruit of the Spirit is charity, joy and peace, patience, understanding of others, kindness and fidelity, gentleness and self-control. (Galatians 5:22–23)

The kingdom of God is not a matter of food or drink; it is justice, peace and joy in the Holy Spirit. . . . (Romans 14:17)

But you, man of God, shun all this. Strive to be holy and godly. Live in faith and love, with endurance and gentleness. (1 Timothy 6:11)

[W]e prove we are true ministers of God in every way by our endurance in so many trials, in hardships, afflictions, floggings, imprisonment, riots, fatigue, sleepless nights and days of hunger.
    People can notice in our upright life, knowledge, patience and kindness, action of the Holy Spirit, sincere love, words of truth and power of God. So we fight with the weapons of justice, to attack as well as to defend. (2 Corinthians 6:4–7)

A person who prays in the Spirit also lives in the Spirit and bears the fruit of the Spirit. Fruits that are delightful to the eyes and sweet to the taste are harvested from a cultivated field or a carefully tended tree. What kind of cultivated field does a person's life have to be to bear such fruit? In his various letters, Paul lists the fruit of the Spirit as love, joy, peace, righteousness, patience, kindness, generosity, faithfulness, gentleness, self-control, and truth-speech.

Paul talks of the *fruit* rather than the fruits of the Spirit because the Spirit produces an ideal portrait of a disciple of Christ. To be a disciple of Christ is the fruit of the Spirit. Just as the Son took flesh by the power of the Spirit, so will disciples be Christ-like in the power of the Spirit. If we use this description of a disciple, a true follower of Christ is one who is peacefully and joyfully ready to welcome others. A disciple of Christ is one who calmly and patiently opens himself or herself to loving others. In other words, a disciple of Christ is a person who gives himself or herself to God and to others in the way Jesus did.

The ideal portrait of the follower of Christ as the fruit of the Spirit also resonates with the manifestations of love that Paul describes in his first letter to the Corinthians: "Love is patient, kind, without envy. It is not boastful or arrogant. It is not ill-mannered nor does it seek its own interest. Love overcomes anger and forgets offenses. It does not take delight in wrong, but rejoices in truth. Love excuses everything, believes all things, hopes all things, endures all things" (1 Cor. 13:4–7). One can even say that the fruit of the Spirit is captured in the one word "love." While there are many gifts that come from the Spirit, Paul tells the Corinthians to strive for the greater gifts. And he shows them a still more excellent way—that of love, the greatest gift of the Spirit. A loving person is the fruit of the Spirit.

For a loving person to be truly the fruit of the Spirit, he or she must love deeply, just as Jesus loved. The Holy Spirit makes Jesus concretely present in the disciples who become Christ-like in love. To pray for the coming of the Spirit is to pray that we become images of Christ. After all, Jesus himself, conceived by the power of the Holy Spirit, was the first fruit of the Spirit. All of us bear within ourselves a mixture of the Spirit and the flesh. We must pray that the Holy Spirit will bear fruit in us so that the Spirit can reap a grand harvest of love.

Three Conditions Essential for Prayer

Praying in the Spirit requires, first of all, *a desire to encounter God*. We can be generous in prayer only if there is an intense desire to meet and encounter God. We begin by praying for a deep desire to see God, knowing that this desire is itself a gift of the Spirit. This is a good beginning; as St. Paul writes, "We do not know how to pray as we ought" (Rom. 8:26). It is the Spirit who leads us to prayer and who will instill a deep desire within us to pray.

Theologian Wilkie Au narrates the story of a student who asked a guru to teach him to pray. The guru led the disciple to a shallow river and plunged the boy's head into the water. (Probably the boy wondered if this was not one of those attention-getting techniques used in seminars.) The guru just kept the student's head under the water until he started to struggle and then the guru let go of him. The boy was bewildered for he went to the guru to be taught a lesson in prayer and not to be killed. The guru then gave the first lesson in prayer. The guru said. "Unless your desire for prayer is as single-minded as your desire for air, you will not succeed." Therefore, the first lesson in prayer is a strong desire to encounter God.

People who are very active in ministry always have reasons to excuse themselves from praying. We priests are often busy and I wonder if many of us still have the desire to pray. The demands of pastoral life often seem to leave us with little time for solitude. What disturbs me greatly is when people find time to go to malls, theaters, and restaurants, but not enough time for contemplation. Why are they able to make time to do these ordinary things but yet excuse themselves from prayer? Perhaps it is not a lack of time but rather a lack of desire.

This is true of so many of us, including families and young people who find time to do many things other than worship and pray. We should pray then for this gift of the Spirit to lead us to prayer.

Unless we have this gift, our efforts will be sporadic, routine, and short-lived. Prayer depends on each individual's desire to encounter God, a desire ignited by the Spirit that leads to stability in prayer.

A second requirement is *humility*. We cannot know the Spirit without humility. I have noted before that humility is letting God be God; humility demands that we let go of our tendencies to control everything. Those in active ministry, whether ordained or non-ordained, are used to being in command. We are great planners, managers, administrators, and visionaries who are always out there and ready to change the world. But there comes a time when we have to let go of the controls and let God be God. The secret lies in allowing ourselves to be blown about as the Spirit wills. Seen this way, humility is not passivity but the readiness to be in harmony with God, to be at God's disposal and service. No wonder truly humble people can be determined and steel-willed.

In humility we should also seek to be transparent in prayer, to encounter the Lord as we truly are. When it comes to prayer and awaiting the Spirit, let us come as our true selves, in our brokenness, tiredness, pains, and sorrow. We should leave behind the selves we wish we were, our fabricated or pseudo-selves. After all, we will be encountering the Spirit of Truth; and so we pray for the gift of transparency before God.

It goes without saying that we need the *disposition of silence* in prayer. What we seek is not the threatening silence of people who do not talk with each other because they are angry. In my experience in leading retreats, sometimes it is not difficult to impose silence on people because part of their lifestyle is a hostile avoidance of neighbors. Silence is nothing new to them and yet this is the noisiest kind of silence, not the kind needed for prayer and nurtured by prayer. Silence is the disposition to wait and to listen with a heightened sensitivity to the Spirit. Those who live by genuine silence become keenly sensitive to other persons and to their needs. They are the "hearts" of the community. Without silence we cannot be sensitive to the stirrings of the Spirit in our hearts, in the hearts of other people, and in the world. Those who learn silence in prayer become effective in discernment and in reading the action of the Spirit in the history of the church, the world, and in their personal lives.

Prayer forms community. True community sustains prayer. Prayer is like a school for community living. Through prayer in the Spirit, we get in touch with our true selves as we also open ourselves to the mystery greater than us. Prayer is a way of being in harmony with God and living by what pleases God. The fruit of prayer is a person of love. The disorder we find in the world comes from a pathetic denial of the truth. We have developed sophisticated ways of covering up evils and producing virtual reality that becomes the norm for truth. Accountability in almost all aspects of life is weak, for there is no higher mystery to which we feel answerable. The fruit is hubris, angst, intolerance, and fear. If people everywhere rediscover prayer and take it to heart, we have a potent force for building a worldwide community.

I want to close this chapter on praying together by narrating an encounter I had with a woman from our parish in Imus, Cavite. It was a gathering of the wives and children of Filipino overseas workers. Her husband was working on a ship that exploded and sank in Norway in early 2004. His body has not been recovered. She said, "Sometimes I tell God that I know my husband is safe somewhere, on an island maybe. They will find him someday. But there are days when a part of me tells God to forgive my husband and grant him eternal rest." As she talked, I could see how her heart was torn between denial and acceptance. She continued, "I go to the Blessed Sacrament but no words come out of my lips. Many times I do not know what to say. I do not know what to pray for. I just catch myself crying before the Lord. My tears—that is the best that I could give God. I trust God will take good care of my children and keep me strong for their sake." With a forced smile to keep her tears from falling, she asked me, "Do you think I am praying?" "Yes," I told her, "you just taught me how to pray."

6

A Community of Hope

Let love be sincere. Hate what is evil and hold to whatever is good. Love one another and be considerate. Outdo one another in mutual respect. Be zealous in fulfilling your duties. Be fervent in the Spirit and serve God.

Have hope and be cheerful. Be patient in trials and pray constantly. Share with other Christians in need. With those passing by, be ready to receive them.

Bless those who persecute you; bless and do not wish evil on anyone. Rejoice with those who are joyful, and weep with those who weep. Live in peace with one another. Do not dream of extraordinary things; be humble and do not hold yourselves as wise.

Do not return evil for evil, but let everyone see your good will. Do your best to live in peace with everybody. (Romans 12:9–18)

One of the most difficult tasks before us today is to convince people to continue hoping in the goodness of each other so they can start anew. Hope is what we also need as a nation, indeed as the family of humanity and creation. Without hope we cannot form community. In a real sense, a community is an achievement of people capable of hope, of believing that goodness is present amidst misery and division.

In the Christian vision, true hope thrives in moments of absurdity and ambiguity, even though in ordinary life it seems our nature to feel more hopeful when things are going well. When the sun is shining, when things are going our way, when we reap the fruits of our labors, when there is harmony within our family, hope is not a problem for us. However, such moments can be frightening because they usually are not true moments of hope. More often they are moments of illusion! The minute a negative experience occurs, the so-called hope easily vanishes, leaving us wallowing in despair, sorrow, or frustration.

Hope in Absurdity

The stories of the great men and women of the old covenant and of the covenant in Jesus speak of how their hope blossomed in moments of absurdity and ambiguity. Abraham, who was promised something absurd, is a good example. "Look up at the sky and count the stars if you can. Your descendants will be like that" (Gen. 15:5). How could he have many descendants when he did not even have one child! How absurd! Sarah laughed. Hers was a logical laugh because she knew she was too old to bear children. For the longest time they waited and their hope was tested. The letter to the Hebrews explains Abraham's stance this way—"By faith he received power of procreation, even though he was too old—and Sarah herself was barren—because he considered him faithful who had promised" (Heb. 11:11). Then Isaac was born. But then God spoke to Abraham once again: "Take your son, your only son Isaac, whom you love, and go to the land of Moriah and offer him there as a burnt offering on one of the mountains I shall point out to you" (Gen. 22:2). Absurd though it was, Abraham did as God said.

For us, living today, Abraham seems more than a bit foolish to have followed God's command (how many of us with children could make this sacrifice?), but that is how it is with those who hope.

They are willing to look absurd to the world as they cling to a promise, or better still, as they trust the One who made the promise. No offer or wish or command is so absurd as to diminish the strength of the given promise for someone who hopes.

Mary is another example of a person facing the absurd. Upon being told that she would bear a son, she asked, "How can this be if I am a virgin?" (Luke 1:34). Then the promise was made to her, "The Holy Spirit will come upon you and the power of the Most High will overshadow you" (Luke 1:35). Again, how absurd! But Mary was also a woman of hope. "I am the handmaid of the Lord, let it be done to me as you have said" (Luke 1:38). She relied completely on the trustworthiness of the Lord who has spoken to her.

Abraham, Sarah, and Mary. Theirs are stories of hope. In times of absurdity and darkness and when logic and human rationality do not seem to provide ready answers, hope with faith comes as the assurance of things not seen. Hope is the assurance that someone dependable has made a promise and shall fulfill it. The promise may seem absurd, but we rely on the one who made it.

In Scriptures it is God who is really the hope-filled one. Scholars say that the theological virtue of hope is directed to God, that the object of hope *is* God, and that we hope *in* God. But as we read the Scriptures, we see that it is really God who hopes in us. It is God who knows how to live with the absurdities of human infidelity and sinfulness and yet continues to hope in us. In the book of the prophet Hosea God is very angry at Israel's forgetfulness. "I loved Israel when he was a child; out of Egypt I called my son. But the more I have called, the further have they gone from me. . . . Yet it was I who taught Ephraim to walk, taking them by the arms; yet little did they realize that it was I who cared for them. I led them with cords of human kindness, with leading strings of love" (Hos. 11:1–4a). After pronouncing the punishment that Israel deserves, God relents. "How can I give you up, Ephraim? Can I abandon you like Admah or make you like Zeboiim? My heart is troubled within me and I am moved to compassion" (Hos. 11:8). It seems absurd that God who knows all things would still trust unfaithful people. But God does.

The New Testament presents many accounts of hope, including the parable of the prodigal son. How could this father continue hoping in a son who squandered everything? Yet he does. And this father serves as a model we should emulate. When a woman anointed the feet of Jesus with expensive perfume, Judas sees only a woman of ill repute. He must have been thinking, "What a waste!" but Jesus, filled with hope, assures those gathered around him, "Truly, I say to you, wherever the Good News is proclaimed, and this will be throughout the world, what she has done will be told in praise of her" (Mark 14:9).

God's hopeful stance is manifested to us through Jesus. It makes communion between God and humanity possible. It is this same hopeful stance that will bring about community among human beings. Jesus formed his first community of disciples purely on the hope that the reign of God could burst forth from the lowly and despised. Community springs forth from hope and a true community brings forth hope. Thus, community is both a fruit and a bearer of hope.

Hope Lies in the "Other"

Hope in community is often experienced when we make room for others. Hope can express itself in the absurdity of making room for others, especially those who differ from us—those on whom we want to close the doors and say, "There is no more room in the inn!" Most of us have plenty of room in our lives but we would rather reserve it for people who will not add discomfort to our existence, which may already be ambiguous or riddled with problems. We want to share space only with those with whom we feel comfortable. But this is how we miss that one element of hope that comes from making room for those whom we do not naturally welcome.

Today, the world finds it increasingly difficult to relate with "the other." Despite massive globalization, we are more ill at ease with diversity. A tendency exists among some people to see as threats those who are "other," those from different cultures and religions or with different languages and mentalities. When problems arise, it is easy to blame the other, and those different from us become easy scapegoats. The problem doesn't stem from us — it stems from them! And yet, the verses from St. Paul's Letter to the Romans encourage mutual love and discourage haughtiness. We need always to fight the tendency to think we are better off as individuals and as communities without "these others." As we eliminate the others from our lives, the others are also eliminating us — and this results in mutual exclusion, which undermines communion and community. When we shut each other out, we eventually sink into despair.

When I became a bishop, I experienced in a more acute way the difficulty of making room for people who differ from me. It has been a genuine exercise in hope to enlarge my heart so I can make room for someone I would not naturally or spontaneously welcome. A bishop's world is cluttered with human encounters — the many liturgies, meetings, congresses, and still more numerous informal exchanges that are part of this life.

I was once involved in a negotiation between factory workers and the management. It was a bitter fight, with both parties hurling accusations at each other. One morning I was scheduled to meet with representatives of the management and their lawyer. My predilection for the poorer and weaker laborers led me to arrive at the meeting with my heart predisposed to labeling management as "the other camp." I resolved not to give them an inch. Every possibility put forth by management to reach a compromise settlement was met with suspicion in my mind. After all, I had already chosen the side of the laborers, and for me management represented "the others."

We finally agreed on a tentative plan and adjourned for lunch. I wanted to beg off, for in my heart and stomach I wondered how I could enjoy a meal with "the others." When the soup was brought in, the lawyer, who had seemed so aggressive during the negotiations, suddenly asked me how he could prepare himself for death. He had cancer and his foremost desire was to be reconciled with God. He talked openly about his failed marriage, his children who had left him, and a new relationship that he wanted blessed in church. Behind the fierce lawyer was a human soul in search of peace, very much like my own soul. He was not an "other" after all. When he shared his deep personal concerns he made room in his heart for me and invited me to enter. But that posed the question of whether I would allow him some room in my heart.

Experiences like this teach me the meaning of hope. Every person encountered is a promise waiting to be fulfilled, a potential source of hope. Fulfillment comes from offering room to and making room for others. Perhaps that other person is looking for that room, or perhaps the other person wants you to share a room in his or her heart. Instead of thinking we are better off without "the others," we should think that we cannot start afresh with life without them. Despite any evidence that shows its absurdity, let us hope in the goodness of each other.

Hope—A Gift of the Spirit

Now, you are the body of Christ and each of you individually is a member of it. So God has appointed us in the Church. First apostles, second prophets, third teachers. Then come miracles, then the gift of healing, material help, administration in the Church and the gift of tongues.

Are all apostles? Are all prophets? Are all teachers? Can all perform miracles, or cure the sick, or speak in tongues, or explain what was said in tongues? Be that as it may, set your hearts on

the most precious gifts, and I will show you a much better way.
(1 Corinthians 12:27–31)

As people of hope we are called to see the good, to see the gift in the other. In this text from chapter 12 of Paul's First Letter to the Corinthians, Paul speaks of his almost mystical vision of the church as the body of Christ. This is a faith vision of a community permeated by the spirit of Jesus and forming the one body who is Jesus the Christ. It is literally a community that is the body of Christ. Within this faith vision, Paul talks about the many gifts of the Spirit that are present in the one body. And what a diversity of gifts! This is undoubtedly because the needs of the body are also diverse. When we follow Paul's mystical vision of this unified community, which is the *totus Christus* (the total Christ), we realize that there is much to celebrate in each other.

When we recognize the gifts of the Spirit, we can celebrate, nurture, and use them to serve the whole body. And we must remember that everyone has received gifts. In the words of the Second Plenary Council of the Philippines, "In the Church, nobody is so poor as to have nothing to give and nobody is so rich as to have nothing to receive." As part of the body of Christ, every person has received a gift from the Spirit, and we need to recognize the unique gift that is present in each person. It is a faith vision of community that will enable us to discern the presence of the gifts of the Spirit in each other, to rejoice and to continue rejoicing. We also acknowledge that no person has a monopoly on all the gifts. This is not negative at all. This limitation enables one to need others and their gifts. This mutual recognition and rejoicing becomes an act of hope in a world of absurd competition that has wasted so many gifts of cultures and of the earth, even destroyed human lives.

While a graduate student in Washington, D.C., I saw an exhibit of Michelangelo's sketches. They were his preliminary studies of projects but even so they were already beautiful and filled with graceful movement. Some pieces showed simply circles, or combinations of them, and yet to my amateur eyes they looked like masterpieces. He was brilliant. After going through the whole exhibit, instead of being hopeful, I felt despair because I was envious. I saw an enormous gift and I did not rejoice in it. I actually felt bad about myself for not possessing a gift like his. At times we are like this. We see a gift and we feel threatened and angry or envious, wondering why that gift was not given to us. My act of despair over the gift of Michelangelo revealed how I have not recognized my own giftedness. In the end, it represented a lack of hope in myself, or of God's hope in me.

A person who approaches the gifts of others begrudgingly or covetously probably does not believe that he or she is equally gifted. It is a form of blindness to the gifts of the Spirit in everyone, including oneself. It is a blindness that leads to despair. Once a seminarian was courageous enough to say to me, "Why do you formators, when guiding us into self-discovery, immediately discover the ugly in us? Then you tell us, 'You'd better fix that. Decide how you will do it.' How will we do it when we are battered, just convinced that there is nothing good in us?!" I thanked that seminarian. It is wiser to start with the giftedness of a person. When the resources are firmly owned, one can be strong to face one's darkness and work to conquer it.

We should celebrate the giftedness of each person and remember that someone else's gift is not a diminution of my own gifts. In fact, the gift of another person honors my giftedness to others. Hope lies within these gifts.

Joining Together in Hope

See, the body is one, even if formed by many members, but not all of them with the same function. The same with us; being many, we are one body in Christ, depending on one another. Let each one of us, therefore, serve according to our different gifts. Are you a prophet? Then give the insights of faith. Let the deacon fulfill his office; let the teacher teach, the one who encourages, convince.

You must, likewise, give with an open hand, preside with dedication, and be cheerful in your works of charity. (Romans 12:4–8)

In the earlier text from his First Letter to the Corinthians, Paul reminds us that we are "parts of one another." We are not only members of the body of Christ but we are also members of one another. It is our union with Christ, in the power of the Spirit that enables us to become members of one another. In chapter 15 of the Gospel of St. John, Jesus says, "I am the vine and you are the branches. As long as you remain in me and I in you, you *bear much fruit*; but apart from me you can do nothing" (15:5). Let us not forget that as we are united with the vine, we are also united with the other branches on that vine. We are connected with the other branches and share in the same life. The life that flows through me is the same life that flows through other people. Indeed, we branches together form the vine. We belong with one another, for better or for worse.

Humanly speaking, one of the most painful things that we could ever hear from another person is the statement "From now on you have no part in me." Sometimes we communicate the sense of this statement without even uttering the words. Instead we communicate by the way we look at one another, by our silence, and by our attitude toward other people: "Hey! You have no part in me. You don't belong with me." This harsh attitude can generate a lot of pain, but it can also be an act of hopelessness. "I do not know what to do with you anymore, so depart from me." What we do not realize is that when we declare people are not part of us, we clip our own wings, deprive ourselves of a shared life, and become incomplete.

In the mystical vision of Paul described in Romans 12, we find our identity by being part of Jesus, by being part of one another, and by being part of this whole beautiful creation. Apart from Jesus, apart from each other, and apart from creation, what are we? We are formed by God to be parts of one another, and to realize this together is to be a community of hope.

Hope is the assurance of God's reliability and trustworthiness despite the absurdities of life and of God's own promises. Hope allows us to experience the fidelity of God despite life's uncertainties and unpredictability. We learn hope from God who sees goodness and charm in us where we only see darkness and sin. If God can hope in us and make room for us, why can we not see beauty in others? Why can we not celebrate each other's giftedness? Why do cultures and nations have to exclude and destroy one another? We need to address these questions as the world becomes unsafe because of our lack of hope in God and in human goodness. Suspicion, self-protection and thirst for domination make the world turn. We are getting dizzy in this maddening frenzy. A community of hope, fruit of Jesus' love and the power of the Spirit, may look absurd to many but it is humanity's hope.

7

A Community of the Holy Spirit

Now, in Christ Jesus, all of you are sons and daughters of God through faith. All of you who were given to Christ through baptism, have put on Christ. Here there is no longer any difference between Jew or Greek, or between slave or freed, or between man and woman: but all of you are one in Christ Jesus. And because you belong to Christ, you are of Abraham's race and you are to inherit God's promise. (Galatians 3:26–29)

In the previous chapters we saw how the triumph of the resurrection includes a new vision of life, of being human and of living together. Faith in the Risen Lord transforms people into a community. The Spirit that is the gift of the Risen Lord sustains that vision of faith, as well as the conditions for making that vision a lived reality. The components of community—sharing, praying, hoping, forgiving, and loving are all human desires, but they are also gifts of Jesus' Spirit. Community is both God's gift and a human responsibility. Women and men at all moments of history long for community yet we realize that it is so hard to achieve and so easy to lose. But to give up working toward its achievement is an irreparable disaster. Especially in our time, the call to community has become more urgent because the promised united humanity has produced instead fragmentation, discrimination, marginalization, ethnic cleansing, confusion and war. The world is crying out for community! And the church, the body of the Risen Christ, animated by the Spirit, has a mission to become a sign of hope. The church is called and challenged by the Risen Lord and the poor of the world to show the path toward community. Composed of believers from various countries, cultures, traditions, languages, and economic standing, the church is in a unique position to manifest how community is possible among such diverse people.

In our world of today, how do we preserve communion and community within the expanding church while respecting diversity? From the time the church first formed, it confronted diversity in cultures, mentalities, lifestyles, and traditions. How did the church, in the power of the Spirit, face such diversity and at the same time preserve the communion that is the gift and identity of the same Spirit? Three illustrations demonstrate how the early church came to appreciate and resolve this question under the guidance of the Holy Spirit.

Diversity in the Early Church

From the history of the early church as reflected in the gospels, the Acts of the Apostles and the epistles, we learn that small local communities formed around the common faith in Jesus the Risen Lord. It could not have been otherwise because personal contact and sharing was the way the disciples spread the faith. The original disciples of Jesus told their stories to a few people, and among those who believed a faith community emerged. As the believers spread to various places, they shared their faith with the people of those places. Small faith communities were born in conditions that differed from each other, even from the context of Jerusalem, the mother church. So then as today there is a church in Thessalonica, a church in Corinth, a church in Rome, a church in Ephesus, a church in Philippi, and churches in others parts of Asia. Each local community was truly church. The church was truly present in each community confessing the one Lord, living by one baptism, nourished by one Word of God and Eucharist, served by one apostolic ministry and committed to the one mission of witnessing to Christ. Each local community was unique yet it was the same church as the other communities. They were bound in communion by the same sacred realities.

The constant exchange between these local churches ensured communion, with mutual recognition and mutual acceptance becoming a way of life. So while separated by thousands of miles and different languages and cultures, they remained one community. From the earliest time, the church has faced questions about communion in diversity within the church. We continue to do so. We need to learn from the early church how to discover the Spirit's work in maintaining unity while respecting diversity.

Acts 6 tells of two groups of Jews, the Hellenists who spoke only Greek and the Hebrews who spoke Hebrew or Aramaic. The Greek-speaking Jews complained that in the distribution of the common goods (*koinonia*) their widows were being neglected. They presented this problem to the apostles, who recognized the injustice of it.

Although we do not know exactly what transpired, Scripture scholars like Raymond Brown have tried to reconstruct the events, looking at all the possible scenarios. Perhaps the Hebrew-speaking group wanted the Greek-speaking group to conform to the Hebrew ways so they would be more Hebrew in language and lifestyle. To achieve this, they deprived the Greek-speakers of access to the common fund. When the problem was presented to the Twelve, the chosen disciples who themselves spoke Hebrew, the Twelve did not automatically side with the Hebrew-speakers. They also refused to handle the common fund. Instead the Twelve allowed the Greeks to choose their own leaders who would help administer the common goods.

This example provides two guides for dealing with diversity. First, very early in its life the church had to deal with a pluralism of cultures and traditions. In the midst of pluralism, the Twelve had to clarify their hierarchy of values. They chose to give the highest value to *koinonia*, the communion arising from the common belief in Jesus Christ. Other differences were secondary. The Twelve respected the differences and let them stand as long as the *koinonia* was preserved.

Second, we learn that Jesus left the disciples with no clear instructions on what to do about practical matters such as caring for the Greek- and Hebrew-speaking widows. It was left to the early church to determine its priorities, establish structures, and find resources to meet its needs, needs that Jesus could not have anticipated during his lifetime. The church existed in many different contexts and in constantly changing circumstances. Fortunately the Holy Spirit, given by Jesus Christ, guides the church in truth and fidelity to Jesus as it faced and continues to face each changing situation.

Another revealing episode in Acts is the story of the conversion of Cornelius. The account in Acts 10:1–48 marks the beginning of the mission to the Gentiles. Cornelius was a Roman centurion, "devout and God-fearing," who had a vision of an angel telling him to send men to Joppa to summon Simon Peter. Later in the story Peter also had a vision. Peter's vision was of a large sheet holding different animals being lowered to the ground and a voice telling him to slaughter and eat the animals. Peter protested because he followed the strict dietary laws of the Jews. The voice told Simon, "What God has made clean, you are not to call profane." Peter did not understand the vision until the men from Cornelius came to him. Later Peter came to understand that the Gentiles have also been given the gift of the Spirit and are thus equally chosen by God.

Good, pious Jews considered the Gentiles so unclean that they would not even enter their houses, lest they be contaminated. But Peter left with the men Cornelius sent and he met with the Roman centurion, a non-Jew, at his house. In Acts 11, Peter explained to those Jews why he had entered the house of a pagan. Peter spoke of his vision and how the Holy Spirit descended upon Cornelius and how Cornelius had listened to him speak of Jesus. Peter told the other Jews, "If, then, God had given them the same gift that he had given us when we believed in the Lord Jesus Christ, who was I to resist God?" The Spirit constantly surprises by making former outsiders true companions, and enemies true neighbors.

A third example appears in Acts 15:1–29 in the account of the assembly that became popularly called the Council of Jerusalem. As followers of the Law of Moses, the Jews had demanded that the Gentiles be circumcised, receiving the mark of the covenant of Abraham, before baptism. This meant that all people had to become Jews and observe the Jewish laws and practices to qualify as Christians. Paul opposed circumcision for all, while Peter favored it. In the end, Peter agreed with Paul that the Greeks, Romans, and other Gentiles did not need to become Jews before baptism because the Spirit can be given and, indeed, had been given also to non-Jews. Faith in the Risen Christ was the primary value. What took precedence was the grace of God in the name of Jesus and in the power of the Spirit.

These three accounts illustrate the difficulties of the early church and its reliance on the Spirit to help it resolve difficulties. When we speak of mission and of both diversity and communion, we are talking about the notion of "catholicity." What do we mean when we say the church is catholic? How can there be one faith that embraces all the different cultures, mentalities, and lifestyles of peoples? When we profess our faith in the "one holy, catholic, and apostolic church," catholicity means both respecting diversity and maintaining communion. To remove diversity is to no longer be catholic.

Diversity and Catholicity

There can be no unity in the church if only one entity or culture dominates while neglecting the others. Nor can unity be achieved by eliminating the many. Although we may be tempted to ignore or push those who differ from us out of the picture, there is no true unity if only like-minded people remain; this is no more than isolation. Instead of eliminating the plural, unity incorporates the plural within a larger whole. This is the meaning of true catholicity.

Unity in the church moves both outwardly and inwardly. This double action of the Spirit was seen in the actions of the apostles. As they extended themselves outwardly, simultaneously there was an impetus to be of one mind and heart, to be interiorly united in faith. Paul sought Peter and the leaders of church to lay before them the gospel he was proclaiming, for he did not want to preach in vain (Gal. 2:2). Paul and Barnabas went to Jerusalem from Antioch in order to report the signs and wonders God had done among the Gentiles. They helped clarify the church's position regarding circumcision of the Gentiles (Acts 15). So from Jerusalem they spread throughout the known world of that time. The churches in these various locations were communities seeking to be united with one another in teaching and in charity; they were not really separated from one another.

The moment we speak of outreach or mission in the church, we open ourselves to diversity and to plurality. The church has long been wary of plurality, and for serious reasons. However, too much caution can sometimes be an obstacle to the growth of the church. If we do no more than begrudgingly admit the uniqueness of people and the differences of their contexts, we do not achieve true catholicity.

One time when I was in a department store in Rome, I overheard voices asking for size six shoes. The two women spoke in English while the saleswoman spoke in Italian. She asked the customers to use the European measuring system, which is different from the American one. Since the customers spoke only English, they did not understand what the Italian woman was asking. As I speak both English and Italian, I intervened with an offer of help.

As one of the customers thanked me, she said, "Why don't all people learn to speak English?" I was amazed: after all, we were in Italy. How would they have felt if the Italian woman had demanded that all people learn to speak Italian if they want to go shopping? If "otherness" is not sufficiently recognized, then the values of uniqueness remain hidden and we cannot appreciate what the others have to offer. Our lives will become poorer.

One summer when I was studying in Washington, D.C., two priests in an Italian parish there went home to Italy. One of the priests picked my name out of a Catholic directory and asked if I could handle a Mass in Italian and if I could, whether I could help out in their parish for five weeks. He told me I could preach in English. The first Sunday I noticed that the parishioners took Italian seriously. The songs and readings were in Italian. These Italian-Americans obviously wanted their children to learn the language, so I decided to preach in Italian. My Italian must have been serviceable because someone even asked for a copy of my homily. Afterward I overheard a woman saying to her grandson, "Look at him. He looks very Asian but he takes the effort to preach in Italian." His grandmother recognized that I was Asian and appreciated that I had done my best to enter her culture. This was a wonderful experience of "otherness" not becoming a block to communion. The differences are acknowledged but brought into a unity of mutual acceptance.

It is sad when a person's "otherness" is not fully appreciated and the person begins to feel worthless. Far too often any culture that wants to be dominant teaches us to believe that we are better off being like "them," rather than remaining "other" than them. In the spirit of Pentecost, the church calls all of us to be one united community in faith and hope. If there is to be an agent of communion between the different cultures of the world, it should be the church. The same Gospel and the same Jesus Christ are expressed in an Indian face, Japanese art, a Filipino smile, an American song, or

European architecture. In the story of the Tower of Babel, one language led to pride. That is a dangerous form of unity. With Pentecost, people of different tongues hear the same message in their own tongue. The unity of arrogance brought about by one language is reversed by the Spirit-filled unity of different languages. "The other" can become a cause of wonder, not of estrangement.

St. Paul's First Letter to the Corinthians has a beautiful description of the church as one body having many members. As there is a diversity of people, so is there a diversity of gifts. While there are many gifts and services within the church there is only one Spirit. The gifts (*charismata*) of the Spirit are the diverse talents or callings to service given to the different members of the body for the common good. A person's gift is to be used to build the community, never to destroy it. The use of the many gifts is encouraged for mutual service and building up of the whole. However, in some cases, the different gifts and ministries lead to scattering. People compete with one another and prevent the gifts of others to flourish. They cannot believe that other people could be as equally gifted as they are. Even in small communities, some members do not respect the gifts of other members. The gifts are wasted, not being able to fulfill the good they could accomplish.

The biblical way of handling the gifts of the Spirit is that they are to be gathered within the community and exchanged with one another. As this gathering and exchange occurs, the individuals within the community are continually aware of the common good, of the unity that encompasses yet transcends all. Gifts are not to be kept hidden and individuals in small communities in the church are to avoid divisiveness. They should promote reciprocity and mutuality in the use of their gifts, becoming agents of mutual service.

Are we at home with our gifts? Our limitations? Do we accept the giftedness and the limitations of others? Are we constantly present to the common good? Are we aware of the impact our division creates among the people we serve? In other words, part of the personal and corporate identity of the Christian is to have a catholic heart, a heart that has room for many different personalities and temperaments and yet brings them together to form a unity. A catholic heart is not threatened by differences. It has room even for enemies. It is the Spirit that is the principal expression of this deep unity in the midst of great diversity. We must pray for the presence of the Spirit because our world needs it, our nation needs it, our church needs it, and our communities and families need it.

Empowered by the Spirit

On the day known as Pentecost, the followers of Jesus had gathered together. Suddenly, there was a noise, a strong driving wind, and tongues of fire appeared (Acts 2:2–3). The Spirit came and with much excitement people heard the saving acts of Jesus announced in their own tongues. Immediately after, Peter addressed the people.

First, Peter assured the people that they were not drunk when they spoke in different tongues. He told the crowd that the action of the Spirit was the fulfillment of the final days as foretold by the prophet Joel (Joel 3:1–5). Peter then proclaimed that the time of salvation had been inaugurated. The last days had come and salvation was near. What the people had been hoping and praying for, that God would intervene in history to bring an end to such a turbulent history, was being fulfilled by the action of the Spirit. This was a tremendous claim for Peter to make, with the memory of the crucifixion and death of Jesus still fresh in people's minds. With the gift of the Spirit Peter was able to see that in spite of the brutality of Jesus Christ's fate, the possibility of new life existed.

With the coming of the Holy Spirit, God inaugurated the time of salvation. It is difficult even for long-time Christians to see that Jesus has truly done this great thing. There are moments when we look at our lives, the state of our nation, the injustice, poverty, and violence around us, and we wonder, "Does Christianity really hold the fulfillment of the promise already begun?" At times it is difficult to believe that human history has been qualitatively changed because of the incarnation, passion, death and resurrection of Jesus. In other words, even Christians find it challenging at times to believe that Jesus *makes* a difference and that Jesus *has made* a difference in the world and in their lives.

The first gift of the Spirit to Peter and the other disciples was a vision of faith—to see the presence of God's saving power at work in history even when or where God seems absent. It is the Spirit who enables people to see fulfillment in broken promises and to see God's fidelity in life's unpredictability. The Spirit beckons us to be like Christ's disciples who sang joyful songs of salvation in the midst of their lamentations. Before Pentecost the disciples saw dangers in being associated with Jesus, and hopes in him dying with his death. The Spirit made the disciples see in faith that God's renewing hand could not be stopped by the destructiveness of the cross.

The second part of Peter's speech focuses on the person of Jesus Christ and the mighty works God accomplished through his life, death and resurrection. It ends with Peter's confession of faith that Jesus is Lord and Messiah. Before the gift of the Holy Spirit, Peter and the other apostles were a timid and fearful group of people. At times they had doubted whether Jesus was truly the one sent by God. Now the gift of the Holy Spirit empowered Peter and his companions to boldly proclaim who Jesus is. If we recall Peter's denial of Jesus and how the other disciples had run away from his company, we appreciate how the Spirit has re-created them into daring witnesses. We are made aware that the church began through the power of the Holy Spirit empowering the disciples to boldly proclaim the Gospel.

At the heart of the birth of the church was the proclamation of the Gospel by the renewed disciples. Before the four evangelists ever began writing, the Gospel was already being proclaimed. This began before and not after the written word. The Gospel already existed with the proclamation of Jesus' identity as Messiah, Lord, and Son of God. The Gospel is both a proclamation and a profession of faith in Jesus that manifests the power and presence of the Spirit.

When I listen to Sunday homilies or Christian education classes, I sometimes wonder if the proclamation and teaching accord with the original inspiration of the Spirit during Pentecost. In some churches, it is common nowadays to hear homilies that do not even mention Jesus Christ. There is timidity, a hesitation, even an embarrassment to proclaim Jesus Christ and what he stood and died for. I recall a parish where I helped out. One of the policies of the pastor was not to mention anything against abortion. When I asked why, the answer was that there might be a parishioner who had had an abortion. I was told that the parish did not want to open old wounds by reminding her of her past, which might stop her from attending Mass. I said that I understood the part about healing wounds of the past. But if the only norm for preaching was to not make people feel uncomfortable with the Gospel, then I could not preach against lying or adultery or injustice or violence or anything else. When I asked what I could preach about, I was told, "Something to make them happy." Is that all there is to Christian preaching? Is the disturbing yet liberating Jesus still at the center of our preaching and of our lives? Is it genuine respect toward people to pretend that we have no need to beg pardon for theft, discrimination, ecological destruction or killing?

One other time I was asked to give an invocation for the opening of a conference, but was told by the organizer not to mention God. I was confused as an invocation is supposed to be a prayer. The explanation was that because some of the participants did not believe in God, they were not to be offended. If that were the case, the organizer should not have included a prayer ritual. Does being aware of other peoples sensibilities curtail us from declaring our faith? Does courtesy toward non-believers mean I have to deny that I am a believer? Do we boldly proclaim Jesus Christ, without being pompous toward those who do not believe in him? Are we apologetic bearers of the Good News who move slowly and softly in case we might offend others?

The Spirit is present in the bold proclamation of the Good News. This is how the Spirit worked in the early church and continues to do so today. I heard a story about Mother Teresa of Calcutta who visited Rome during an international retreat. One of the priest-observers asked her, "What can we priests do to help in your apostolate?" Mother Teresa was quiet for some time until she said, "One thing: Give us Jesus, only Jesus, always Jesus." And that was how the church began—only Jesus, always Jesus—receiving Jesus in faith, sharing Jesus in love.

The third part of Peter's speech (Acts 2:38–40) addressed the needs of the people who wanted to know what they were to do to follow Jesus. Peter answered that they must repent or undergo *metanoia*, which many translate as conversion. They were to change their way of thinking, of perceiving, of looking at reality. And this has value for those of us who are already baptized Christians. "Being Christian" does not mean being a bona fide registered member of the church with no urgent need to change our way of looking at reality. All the baptized need constant *metanoia*, a "change of mind," to put on the mind of Christ. Some people who think they are already close to God are often the ones who find it most difficult to change their ways of thinking according to the Gospel. The Holy Spirit helps us change our vision of the world, humanity, and society and attune it to the will of God; without the Spirit's guidance, we may fool ourselves into doing our own will instead of God's will.

Finally, Peter promised the gift of the Holy Spirit to those who were baptized, to their children, and "to all those far off, whomever the Lord our God will call." For a Jew, this promise was subversive because the original Pentecost celebrated the birth of Israel, God's chosen people, after liberation from slavery. Now Peter is saying that the Spirit is promised to all who believe in Jesus Christ.

The Spirit is promised even to "those far off." They now belong to God's people.

People who have received the Spirit should not consider themselves superior to those yet to receive the Spirit. The Spirit that they receive will be the same Spirit everyone else receives, making everyone equal. From the beginning, then, the grace of the church is to be inclusive and egalitarian. No one is excluded, all are welcomed, and everyone is equal because of the gift of the Spirit. At times we forget that the Spirit is the foundation of inclusiveness and equality in a community. Many times we get lost in our different roles and functions and the distinctions between ranks. If we take these things too seriously and fight over them, we can lose sight of the Spirit working in our midst. Unconsciously we might start dividing people between those who have access to the Spirit and those who do not according to their social or ecclesiastical standing.

Once a group of potential benefactors visited our seminary in Tagaytay located in the mountains south of Manila. When I opened the door, some seminarians went out to greet them. As they were talking, one seminarian tried to introduce me but I motioned him not to bother as everyone was enjoying the conversation. Then one of the benefactors turned to me in a patronizing way, "Do you also need a benefactor?" The seminarians started laughing and one said, "He is the rector." When they heard I had the top position in the seminary, everything changed. In their eyes I was transformed from being a person who might need them to someone they now need because as a priest, I am "close to God." Titles and ranks are so embedded in our mentality that a title can immediately raise a person on a pedestal. This can be a source of great temptation for us, especially for clergy and parish leaders.

The Spirit came as a tempest of wind and fire to give birth to a wonderful creation called church, boldly proclaiming Jesus as Christ, Lord, and Son of God. The Spirit's presence is felt in each of us today as we constantly change our way of thinking to remain open to do the will of God. In one of its beautiful prayers, the church begs the Holy Spirit to fill our hearts and to renew the face of the earth. We need an outpouring of the one we invoke as "creator blest" for the church and for the world.

The church, creation of the Spirit to be a sign of humanity's communion with God and communion among human beings, does not always live up to its calling. The division between Christians is a counter-witness to the unifying action of the Spirit. The prejudice and animosity of some Christians toward non-Christians do not mirror the reconciling power of the Spirit. The sexual and financial scandals associated with the clergy have caused bitterness and distrust. The lack of genuine dialogue between pastors and laity, between bishops and priests, between lay leaders and between local churches stifles the integrating movement of the Spirit. We ask pardon of the Spirit, the church, and humanity for these shortcomings. We should heed the call of the Spirit for the church to be a sign of what our contemporary world longs for—hope for wholeness, unity in diversity, boldness in faith, and universal love. Come Holy Spirit, in our hearts take up your rest!

8

Reaching Out

A Christian community does not exist for its members only. It exists for the whole world, for the whole of humanity. It exists for mission. The action of the Spirit within the church enables the church to affirm and promote the stirrings of the same Spirit in the world.

As a Christian community forms, space must always be set aside for the quiet miracles of the Spirit. The Spirit of Jesus can be present even in the most broken of persons and in spite of their very natures. It may take some work for the Spirit's consoling presence to be discerned and believed in the midst of personal troubles and troubles at the workplace or in our society. Today it seems increasingly difficult to witness a covenant resting on common humanity, but such a covenant needs to be forged again with renewed vigor.

For this to happen, the church must spearhead a movement toward constructive tolerance, which goes beyond a reluctant accommodation of differences. The Spirit seeks a calm and joyful recognition and integration of other systems of meanings or cultures, allowing them to build up the whole. This inclusiveness is an indispensable element of the church's life and mission.

Respect for human dignity is central to true solidarity. Among the many people who do not experience solidarity are the minority groups in various countries. They are the migrant workers, the culturally and socially voiceless, the economically deprived, and the displaced peoples. In our fragmented world of minorities, the church has a privileged opportunity to witness to the grace-filled love of God that sees human beings as they are rather than seeking out any lovable qualities they have to offer or from which one could profit. This grace-filled love, known as *agape*, is the soul of mission. The power of this love impels the church to be of service everywhere to people as people, to really exist for people, even those outside its fold, to be a universal sacrament for the world. The mission of solidarity requires seeing a neighbor in "the other," in a wounded "foreigner," in the "Samaritan" (Luke 10:25–37).

Solidarity with those who are "other" or those who are minorities becomes solidarity with all peoples, especially the suffering and victims. Solidarity, however, becomes truly dynamic only when it breaks down barriers that stand in the way of peace. It is commonplace to think of serving minorities throughout the world in terms of kind acts that are necessary and laudable. But we cannot and should not allow the church to treat minorities or "others" simply as beneficiaries of the church's charity or goodness. Reaching out in solidarity can be jarring and messy at times. At times we may feel that it is too heavy a burden for us. That is when we should recall God's solidarity with us through the Incarnation, when Jesus became one of us.

The Incarnation does not mean that Jesus simply assumed a human body. The assumption of the human body for Jesus meant that God became entangled in this mess called human existence. Jesus' identification and solidarity with the human condition—its problems, longings, sufferings, failures, dreams, and hopes—is a missionary element of the Incarnation. The Incarnation of Jesus is a call to us to get involved in human things.

Peruvian theologian Gustavo Gutiérrez has said that mission is tied to more than a geographic space. For example, the men and women of the Philippine church are constantly challenged to be missionaries in Asia. Asia, though, is not just a geographic space where you can say, "I've been to Bangkok. I was in Hong Kong. I was in China." If you do, then you were merely a tourist, not a missionary. Father Gutiérrez rightly notes that mission must tie Christians, just like Jesus, to *human* space because that is the very principle of the Incarnation. This is the reason why in *Ecclesia in Asia* (the apostolic exhortation after the Special Assembly of the Synod of Bishops for Asia held in 1998) the Holy Father and the bishops of Asia depicted Asia not only in terms of place, but also in terms of the longings, thirst, hunger, dreams, values, history, and heritage of a people. If any church wants to follow the mission of Jesus, it must reveal a God-in-this-world, for many people feel that God does not care, that God is silent, or that God has abandoned human beings.

A few years ago, a beggar appeared at the door of our seminary in Tagaytay. The man was very dirty and he carried a baby sucking from a bottle of what looked like dirty, brownish water. I could tell the baby was very hungry from the way it sucked at the bottle with full force. It was so innocent that it probably did not know the difference between milk and dirty water. When the man stood outside my window I asked where he was from. He said, "I'm here from Payatas. We lost our house." (Payatas is an open garbage pit north of Manila where a community of scavengers live. Not long ago an avalanche destroyed houses and buried whole families alive.) He had come to Tagaytay to look for his siblings but he did not know where they were living. I asked him, "Do you want to eat?" "Yes, I want to eat," he said, and then he asked me, "Are you a priest?" I replied, "Yes." "Father, where is God?" I did not know how to answer him so I tried to avoid the question by saying, "Somebody will come with your food."

My encounter with that man was an invitation to mission. Could I get involved? Could I cross the window that divided me from this victim? Could I leave my room and somehow, even just for a few minutes, get involved? I may not be able to solve his problem but can I somehow be a mirror of the God who in Jesus is involved in the dreams of the people? It is not so much my being able to do something but my being in solidarity with God's people. The mission of Jesus is to make God known as the God who *is* involved in human history.

> *This is what has been from the beginning, and what we have heard and have seen with our own eyes, what we have looked at and touched with our hands, I mean the Word who is Life....*
>
> *The Life made itself known, we have seen Eternal Life and we bear witness, and we are telling you of it. It was with the Father and made himself known to us.*
>
> *So we tell you what we have seen and heard, that you may be in fellowship with us, and us, with the Father and with his Son, Jesus Christ.*
>
> *And we write this that our joy may be complete.* (1 John 1:1–4)

This familiar text is a beautiful summary of how Christian mission began with an experience. It began with someone who had seen, touched and heard Jesus, the Incarnate One, and who had seen, touched, and heard the Father in Jesus. That experience was a gripping experience of faith, an experience that turned an ordinary person into an apostle. Such an experience is the essence of an encounter with the Risen Lord, like the one that transformed a timid Peter into a courageous apostle. It is this absorbing experience that transformed Paul the persecutor into the greatest apostle to the Gentiles.

Christian mission ultimately arises from a deep experience of the God revealed by Jesus. Not the God that we have read about nor the God that I have heard others talk about, but the God that I have seen, touched and heard—the God revealed by the Incarnate

One. Knowing this God can transform me. It can make me an apostle. It can make me a missionary with a very simple plan: not to conquer the world but simply to narrate my story so that those who hear of my experience may be drawn to the same experience.

When you have good news coming from a lived encounter, no one has to tell you to proclaim it—the very power of the experience impels you to do so. In the words of St. Paul, "Woe to me if I keep quiet." This is Good News, and this is so good that I cannot keep it to myself. I must go around running, walking, even kneeling to tell it so that other people may also experience it. From this shared experience will spring our communion with God in Jesus Christ.

As we reach out in mission we must believe that we bear in our hands, hearts, and in our very persons the true power of the Risen Lord, the full power given to him by God. This is not to engage in false grandeur but to develop a sense of responsibility for the community that is healed by the Lord's power. The horizon of our mission is very wide because it corresponds to the all-embracing authority and power of Jesus. From the lost sheep of Israel, Jesus now sends the disciples to all nations and to all strata of human life. But they must go out. Disciples cannot sit and wait around for the people to come to them. Jesus tells us to go to the people, to go out to them and teach them.

We will not be teaching anything new. Jesus has already given us what we are to teach. There are those of us who think, "Oh, this is getting to be boring! Let's teach something new," but the Risen Lord tells us not to invent new teachings. "Teach them to fulfill all that I have commanded you" (Matt. 28:20). Our mission is to keep the memory of Jesus alive in us and to constantly draw from this rich well of memory. We will not be preaching our own ideas or our own doctrines. We will be preaching Jesus and everything he has left us, drawing from the "old" what is ever new.

And Jesus will always be with us. A beautiful promise closes the Gospel of Matthew: "I am with you always until the end of this world" (Matt. 28:20). It reminds us of the promise at the beginning of Matthew, *"The virgin will conceive and bear a son, and he will be called Emmanuel* which means God-with-us" (1:23). This is so like the promise of the Risen Christ, "I am with you (Emmanuel) always." The resurrection gives us the abiding presence of Jesus Christ. God is irrevocably with us. His is not a transitory presence — one day here, the next day gone, and then here again. God's presence is forever abiding.

Witness without Fear

> *Thomas, the Twin, one of the Twelve, was not with them when Jesus came. The other disciples told him, "We have seen the Lord." But he replied, "Until I have seen in his hands the print of the nails, and put my finger in the mark of the nails and my hand in his side, I will not believe."*
>
> *Eight days later, the disciples were inside again and Thomas was with them. Despite the locked doors Jesus came and stood in their midst and said, "Peace be with you." Then he said to Thomas, "Put your finger here and see my hands; stretch out your hand and put it into my side. Resist no longer and be a believer."*
>
> *Thomas then said, "You are my Lord and my God."* (John 20:24–28)

This account of the fear and doubt of Thomas signals the support we will have. Jesus' Spirit will strengthen our capacity to share with others the Good News. When others receive our testimony, it will be as if the Risen Christ is before them. The early church evolved as a community through this simple sharing between witness and hearer. The witness testified to his or her experience of the Risen Lord and the hearers received the testimony. As they shared and received each other's testimonies there was communion between them, and this communion was communion with God. The genesis of the church was and is a resurrection event.

Once a week we have a prayer meeting in the seminary in Tagaytay. In some parishes Bible-sharing groups in the neighborhoods gather once a week to reflect on the Sunday Gospel. Sometimes the sharing becomes very abstract or academic instead of experiential. The prayer meeting turns into an ordinary meeting. People seem embarrassed to share their personal encounters and relationships with Christ in their prayer experiences. But when some people dare to truly witness to their lived encounter with the Risen Lord, the atmosphere changes. The hearts of the listeners burn within them and they share from their hearts' memories too. How can we build a community if not on the basis of our personal relationship with Christ?

Street or public preaching is not uncommon in the Philippines. There have been occasions on the bus from Cavite to Manila when someone will suddenly start preaching, "This is the day the Lord has made. Let us rejoice!" and later pass a bag for donations. Although I disagree with some of their interpretations of Scripture, I cannot help but admire their enthusiasm and willingness to undergo humiliation at the hands of indifferent passengers. Because of this, I occasionally donate some money. After one such experience, I told the seminarians, "I'm thinking of sending you out on the public buses to start preaching." The seminarians were upset: "Father, stop joking!" I said, "No! I'm serious!" "Please, Father, don't! It's embarrassing!" But these "bus evangelists" were preaching the Word of God. Someone else on that same bus might have been touched by their words or the message read from the Gospels and the letters of Paul.

Italian theologian Severino Dianich said that belonging to a church means being able to share a personal experience with the living Lord and receiving the sharing of someone else's experience with the living Lord. If all we know about the church are the rituals, the Scriptures, the rules, then we do not know what it means to belong to a church. Therefore, to say "I know what it means to belong to a church" is to stake a very powerful claim.

It is to claim that you have a relationship with others centered on the experience of the Risen Lord—testimony given and testimony received.

I remember a simple yet fascinating experience of church because of testimony given and received. In a seminar to combat corruption in society that I attended, we listened to the story of a woman working as an auditor of government offices. She discovered an anomalous transaction involving millions of pesos. With data uncovered by investigations, a case was filed against some influential people. It did not take long for the accused to try to bribe her. Just for absenting herself from every court hearing, she was offered half a million pesos. Two absences would make her an instant millionaire. What an offer! At that time her mother was sick and needed money. Fear and doubt crept in. But she prayed. She turned down the offer, pursued the case and risked her life. She attributed her determination to faith, to a conviction that the Lord was with her and blessed the just act that she was doing. It was her way of saying, "My Lord and my God!" The group attending the seminar received her testimony and we were confirmed in our own faith that the Risen Lord is truly at work! A community of common commitment has arisen. The Risen Lord is renewing his church again.

We are thankful for doubting Thomas because he leaves with us the highest expression of faith in Jesus, "My Lord and my God." Thomas recovers from his doubt when he encounteres the Lord himself. His personal experience of the Risen Christ transformed him from a doubter setting precise conditions for belief ("*Unless* I see the mark of the nails in his hands and put my finger in the mark of the nails and my hand in his side, I will not believe") to a personal witness (*My* Lord and *my* God!). Thomas' proclamation has become the church's confession of faith from generation to generation—the Risen One is truly Lord and not only Lord, but also truly God.

Conclusion

Today there are many ways of saying "God," of confessing Jesus as Lord and God, of letting others know of the active presence of God in the world. In the life of the early church, saying "God" was the domain of the bishops—the episcopal setting. Then the monastic setting became the place for saying "God." Later the great universities and, after Trent, the seminaries became the places to say "God." Today, so many different places are saying "God"—in every country, in large and small churches, in villages and small basic Christian communities. It is essential that Christians today not forget to say "God," lest the world forget and believe that God is no longer present or is even superfluous. Saying "God" isn't easy at times. It can be quite risky.

For most people today, the world of elite globalization represents a futureless growth because it is growth without jobs, and it is growth that destroys the environment, putting into serious peril the existence of quality life in the future. It can also be rootless growth because it is growth that cuts us from the roots of our values and traditions. And it can be a meaningless growth because many times people lose their direction in life. In the midst of all these challenges, the world is convincing us to forget our neighbor, to forget God, all in the name of profit and competition. It is not easy to say "God" in a world that wants to forget that neighbors exist.

Three years ago, just after I was ordained bishop, the special novena masses, *Simbang Gabi*, attended at dawn by Filipinos in preparation for Christmas, had already started. After celebrating the Eucharist in the cathedral and still wearing my full vestments, I greeted the people as they went out the door. As I stood there, I saw that little children were selling flowers and impeding the progress of the people leaving the church. *"Bulaklak po! Bulaklak!*

Bulaklak!" (Flowers! Flowers! Flowers!) I ran after them, scolding them until we reached the road. I was still in my full regalia as I shouted at those children, "Look, we have not forbidden you from selling flowers but let us put some order here! You can sell flowers here at the gate. The people who are attending Mass and the people who are leaving the church will certainly pass through the gate."

All the children were trembling before me in fear. I spotted the tallest girl. "You! How old are you?" She softly said, "Fourteen." I replied, "You see! You're fourteen years old. Is it difficult to understand what I'm saying? That you can sell at this point and not beyond it?" And she answered, "No. I understand."

Then I looked at the smallest boy, a very dirty-looking boy. "You! How old are you?" He looked up, smiled and said, "Seven." I said, "You're seven years old. Can you understand what I'm saying?" It was then that he hugged me. He was so small that his hands only reached my waist. He hugged me and again smiled the sweetest smile. He started stroking my back and gently said, "Father, *Obispo ka na. Obispo ka na*" (Father, you are now a bishop). I stopped and I said, "Yes." God was calling me again and asking me to utter "God" to these children in compassion.

I have never sold flowers, or anything else for that matter. I have never wanted for anything; as a child, all I had to do was go to school. These children have to work every day, including Sunday, to have something. There I was, uttering laws, policies, the need for order, and cleanliness. And this young boy uttered a word addressed to my heart, to my identity.

For the next half hour, I just stayed with the children at the gate, still in my full vestments, and had a grand time talking with them. Those children taught me how to listen to God and how to say "God."

The following Saturday, I was invited to bless a chapel, where I had first been assigned as a young priest and pastor. The priest there suggested that we could use the occasion for a pastoral visit, not the formal visit where the bishop looks at the books and the accounts but just a friendly visit. I accepted because it was also an occasion for me to see my former parishioners.

When I arrived at the site of the new chapel, the bands were playing and I was given a large key to the town. As I entered the chapel, I saw the elderly woman who used to take care of us in 1982. After Mass, she always served us coffee and *pan de sal*. I approached her and said in jest, *"Lola Juana! Buhay pa pala kayo!"* (Grandmother Juana! You are still alive!) She grabbed my hand and said, "You still remember me. You still know my name." Then she said, "I'm dying of cancer. I have not been home here for years. Now I live in Manila to be close to the hospital but when I learned that you were coming here as a bishop, I forced my nieces and nephews to take me." She added, "It was worth it. It was worth the travel and all the pain. You still know me. You still know my name." Still holding my hand, she put it near her breast and said, "Pray to God. Pray that I may be healed." Within me were protests, "I cannot heal you. I cannot." Yet she was looking at me in total faith, believing that somehow, through this thin bishop, God would hear her.

At the end of the Mass, I could not leave the chapel. People crowded around me—in front of me, behind me, to my left, my right, even above me. I even saw a little boy trapped below me. I pleaded with the people, "Please give this small boy enough space." Then an elderly woman spoke up, "We apologize, Bishop! But you are the first bishop I have seen and I will probably not see a bishop again in my life. Please don't deny me this opportunity."

In these simple ways, people said "God."

Listen to people saying "God." Learn from the people, the forgotten ones, your neighbors. Remember that *our* way of saying "God" is not the *only* way. Learn from them. Learn from the victims of senseless violence and suffering. Learn how they say "God" in hope. Learn from those pushed to the limits of the paradox of saying "God," those who sometimes leave it unsaid but never forget God. Learn from them. We must continue saying "God" with all the joys and pains and risks it involves. Continue saying "God" with all the praise and lament it invites. Continue saying "God" with all the silence that that mystery creates and evokes. Continue saying "God." Continue forming and living Christian community in love, in prayer, in solidarity, and in hope.

✦ ✦ ✦

Heavenly Father, how can we thank you enough? The Risen One, your Son, who continues to form us into the sons and daughters that you deserve, appears to us. He accompanies us in our frustrations. He accompanies us when we are weeping, running around, looking for the dead. He accompanies us in our humiliations. He accompanies us in our work places. He accompanies us as the Risen Lord, inviting us to share in his new life so that a new history may be born for us, for our families, for our communities, for our nation, for our world.

We will never be able to fathom this mystery, but one thing is sure — what matters is for us to live the new histories and the new mission that the Risen One offers us. Open our hearts. Make us generous. Form in us the eagerness of Mary Magdalene. Form in us the humility of Peter. Form in us the burning hearts of the disciples on their way to Emmaus. Then, maybe, even outside the Easter season, we will proclaim in word and in deed, and in mission, "We have seen the Lord. It is the Lord!" Amen.

About the Author

Bishop Luis Antonio G. (Chito) Tagle, of the Diocese of Imus, Cavite, Philippines, finished his theological and graduate studies at the Loyola School of Theology (Manila) and The Catholic University of America (Washington, D.C.). Prior to his Epis-copal ordination in 2001, he was a member of the Vatican's International Theological Commission.

Bishop Tagle is pastor of Our Lady of the Pillar Cathedral (Imus). He continues to be rector of Tahanan ng Mabuting Pastol (Tagaytay City) and a consultant to the Philippines bishops' commissions on the Doctrine of the Faith and on Seminaries. He is also a member of the Editorial Board of *Storia del Concilio Vaticano II, Instituto per le scienze religiose* (Bologna). He is a much sought-after speaker and retreat director in the Philippines, throughout Asia, and abroad. He continues to teach systematic theology at the Loyola School of Theology, Ateneo de Manila University.

www.ingramcontent.com/pod-product-compliance
Lightning Source LLC
Chambersburg PA
CBHW070202100426
42743CB00013B/3013